IRISH
COOKING

IRISH COOKING

VIVIENNE ABBOTT

THE GOLDSMITH PRESS

IRELAND 1987

A GOLDSMITH book published by
The Goldsmith Press Ltd.
Newbridge Co. Kildare Ireland
and distributed by
Overseas Publications Ltd.
Broombridge Road Dublin 11

Second edition The Goldsmith Press 1987

ISBN 0904984 99 0 (Paper)
      0904984 98 2 (Cloth)

Designed by Anna Read

Colour photography by David Davies

Drawings by Leslie Forbes

Filmset by Inforum Ltd. Portsmouth Hampshire

CONTENTS

Acknowledgements

To Mrs Maura Hastings of Easons in Dublin for continuous support and encouragement; to all my colleagues and friends, especially Jim Kilbride and Anna Barron from the Dublin College of Catering; to Gearóid O Maolcraoibhe who clarified historical points; to Colm Duggan of the Research Department of Fisheries in Dublin who generously shared his enthusiasm and encyclopedic knowledge of Irish fish with me; to Sean McMorrow of the Inland Fisheries Trust; to Aideen Foley of Guinness's; to Liam Miller of the Dolmen Press and his wife Joe; to the Goldsmith Press and Desmond Egan for permission to quote from his poem 'Perch' in *Midland* (The Goldsmith Press, Curragh, Kildare); to Dr Peter Kavanagh of New York for permission to quote his brother's poem 'Restaurant Reverie' in *Complete Poems* (The Peter Kavanagh Hand Press, New York); to Ina Manahan (Journey's End, Crookhaven, Goleen, West Cork) for the recipe Journey's End Chicken; to Gerry and Mary Galvin of the Vintage Restaurant in Kinsale; to Desmond Moran of Knockferry House in Co. Galway; to Mrs Egan and Mrs Keating of Kilkee and to Chris Garde of the Ashbourne House Hotel in Co. Cork.

British/American Equivalent Measures and Terminology

British	American
ALMONDS	
Whole Blanched 4 oz	$\frac{3}{4}$ cup
Ground 2$\frac{1}{2}$ oz	$\frac{1}{2}$ cup
BREADCRUMBS	
Fresh 2 oz	1 cup
Dried 2 oz	$\frac{3}{4}$ cup
BUTTER, MARGARINE AND WHITE FATS	
$\frac{1}{2}$ oz	1 tablespoon
$\frac{3}{4}$ oz	1$\frac{1}{2}$ tablespoons
1 oz	2 tablespoons
1$\frac{1}{2}$ oz	3 tablespoons
2 oz	4 tablespoons
2$\frac{1}{2}$ oz	5 tablespoons
3 oz	6 tablespoons
4 oz	$\frac{1}{2}$ cup
5 oz	$\frac{5}{8}$ cup
6 oz	$\frac{3}{4}$ cup
8 oz	1 cup
CEREALS	
3 oz oatmeal	1 cup
CHEESE	
Grated	
$\frac{1}{2}$ oz	2 tablespoons
1 oz	$\frac{1}{4}$ cup
2 oz	$\frac{1}{2}$ cup
4 oz	1 cup
CREAM	
2 fl. oz	4 tablespoons or $\frac{1}{4}$ cup
3 fl. oz	6 tablespoons
4 fl. oz	$\frac{1}{2}$ cup
$\frac{1}{4}$ pint (5 fl. oz)	$\frac{5}{8}$ cup
$\frac{1}{2}$ pint	1$\frac{1}{4}$ cups
1 pint	2$\frac{1}{2}$ cups
CRAB	
4 oz	$\frac{1}{2}$ cup
8 oz	1 cup
DRIED FRUIT	
Currants, Raisins, Sultanas	
1 oz	2 tablespoons
2 oz	$\frac{1}{3}$ cup packed
4 oz	$\frac{2}{3}$ cup packed
6 oz	1 cup packed
EGG WHITES	
1 egg white, large	2 tablespoons
4 egg whites, large	$\frac{1}{2}$ cup
FLOUR, PLAIN/ALL PURPOSE	
(sifted before being measured)	
$\frac{1}{2}$ oz	2 tablespoons

1 oz	4 tablespoons
2 oz	good $\frac{1}{2}$ cup
3 oz	good $\frac{3}{4}$ cup
$3\frac{1}{2}$ oz	1 cup
4 oz	1 cup and 2 tablespoons
8 oz	$2\frac{1}{4}$ cups
1 lb	$4\frac{1}{2}$ cups

HONEY, JAM, SYRUP, PRESERVES
4 oz	$\frac{3}{8}$ cup
6 oz	$\frac{1}{2}$ cup
8 oz	$\frac{3}{4}$ cup
12 oz	1 cup
1 lb	$1\frac{3}{8}$ cups

ICE CREAM
6 oz	1 cup

LOBSTER
4 oz	$\frac{1}{2}$ cup
8 oz	1 cup

MEAT
Diced Cooked Meat
3 oz	$\frac{1}{2}$ cup
6 oz	1 cup
8 oz	$1\frac{1}{3}$ cups

NUTS
Large
2 oz shelled	$\frac{1}{2}$ cup (generous)
4 oz shelled	1 cup (generous)

Ground
2 oz	$\frac{1}{2}$ cup
4 oz	1 cup

SUGAR
Caster/Granulated
1 oz	1 tablespoon
2 oz	$\frac{1}{4}$ cup
3 oz	$\frac{1}{3}$ cup
4 oz	$\frac{1}{2}$ cup
5 oz	$\frac{2}{3}$ cup
6 oz	$\frac{3}{4}$ cup
7 oz	bare 1 cup
8 oz	1 cup

Fresh Fruit and Vegetables

APPLES
1 lb apples, sliced	$2\frac{2}{3}$ cups
1 lb cooking apples	3 medium size

CUCUMBER
1 British	2 American

MUSHROOMS
$\frac{1}{2}$ lb fresh sliced	$2\frac{1}{2}$ cups
$\frac{1}{2}$ lb fresh diced	2 cups

ONIONS

½ lb sliced	2 cups
1 lb sliced	4 cups
8 oz chopped	1 cup

SHALLOTS

1 medium shallot finely chopped	1 tablespoon
2 oz	½ cup

SOFT FRUITS

Sold in America as pints or quarts – 4 cups = 1 quart

Raspberries 5 oz	1 cup
Redcurrants 4 oz	1 cup
Blackcurrants 4 oz	1 cup
Blackberries 4 oz	1 cup
Strawberries 6 oz	1 cup

TOMATO

1 lb tomatoes	3 – 4 medium American tomatoes
1 lb fresh tomatoes, peeled, seeded, juiced and chopped	1½ cups tomato pulp

TURNIPS

1 lb peeled and quartered	2½ cups

WATERCRESS

1 bunch	1½ cups

British/American Terminology

Ingredients

Almonds, ground	Almonds, finely ground
Beef stock cube	Beef bouillon cube
Cornflour	Cornstarch
Crayfish	Crawfish
Cream, double	Whipping or heavy
Cream, single	Light
Egg, white of	Egg white
Fats, cooking (i.e., white vegetable fat)	Shortening
Flour, plain	All purpose
Flour, self raising	Self rising
Hazlenuts	Cob nuts or filberts
Pepper, freshly milled	Freshly ground
Potatoes, creamed	Potatoes, mashed
Prawns	Shrimps
Stock	Broth – Bouillon
Suet, shredded beef	Chopped beef suet
Sultanas	Seedless white raisins
Tomato purée concentrate	Tomato paste

Sugar

Caster or granulated	Granulated

Fresh Fruit and Vegetables

Apples, cooking	Green apples
Onion, Spanish	Spanish or Bermuda
Onion, spring	Scallions or green

INTRODUCTION

A half-potato on my plate
It is too soon to celebrate
The centenary of '48
Or even '47.
You're boasted to the centre, too,
And wet, in soapy soil you grew,
But I am thankful still to you
For hints of history given.

There's something lonely far away
In what you symbolise to-day
For me – the half that went astray
Of life, the uncompleted.
But up brown drills new pink buds start
With truer truth than truth of art,
Ignoring last crop's broken heart
And a generation defeated.
O here is life
Without a wife
A half-potato, eat it.

'Restaurant Reverie' from *Complete Poems* (The Peter Kavanagh Hand Press, New York)

Patrick Kavanagh's poem may be ironic in tone – yet he finds no difficulty in allowing a special symbolism to the lowly potato (and a soapy one at that, not even the usual 'ball of flour'). In this he shows himself a true Irishman, for the Irish have always had a slant of their own in the matter of food. In the earliest days of what could be called Irish society, the question of what food and hospitality should be offered to visitors assumed such importance that it was covered by special legislation under the old Brehon Laws: not surprising, perhaps, in a country to become famous as 'a land flowing with milk and honey'. It is of course true that there were a number of famines in Ireland during the nineteenth century – one in 1847 a calamity of horrific proportions – yet it would seem that politics played almost as big a part here as did the failure of the potato crop to which Kavanagh refers in his poem. And in modern times, as in days of old, the Irish are arguably the best-fed race in the world. The mild, damp climate gives to our pasture land a green lushness all the year round, continually astonishing visitors. It is still not unknown – and it was quite common in earlier centuries – for many domestic animals to be left outside throughout the winter.

At its best, Irish food is plain and wholesome, leaving its ingredients to speak for themselves. Their quality has always been, and still is, the cornerstone of Irish cooking. If our cuisine is limited, the fault certainly does not lie in the ingredients. A chauvinist might even go so far as to argue that these are so good as to reduce the need for fancy dishes – but then, we have our fair share of these too, as I hope the reader will discover. Perhaps the account of Bricriú's legendary feast is relevant here: he tells us, for example, of the boar served up which 'since it was a piglet had eaten nothing but fresh milk, porridge and meal in spring, pure cream and milk in kernels of nuts and pure wheat in autumn, and milk and broth in winter.' Milk-fed calves and cattle fed only on fresh milk, sweet meadow-hay and corn were also esteemed. The famous twelfth-century chronicler, Giraldus Cambrensis, tells us that the deer which teemed in Irish forests were so fat that they could not run too fast and so were very easy game. Things had not changed much by 1672 when a French visitor could declare categorically: 'This is a land of plenty'. Around the same time the Papal Nuncio Cardinal Rinnucini, whatever his reservations about the climate, and indeed about some of the natives, was very impressed with the fare: plenty of fruit, apples, pears, plums and artichokes. He found the food incredibly cheap – he could, for example, buy one thousand oysters for one shilling. God be with the days!

As might be expected of an island, fish here has always been plentiful and an extremely important part of the Irish diet; until recently, thanks to Roman Catholic Canon-law, it provided the main course on most tables for Friday dinner, and still probably figures in a meal once a week. Geographers today explain the seas' bounty as being in large part due to the Continental Shelf and the warm Gulf Stream, but in other times the extraordinary richness of the Celtic Sea could only be explained as miraculous. So it was believed that St Patrick had blessed the river Moy with the result that it became the milch-cow of the waters of Ireland, for in it fish is caught all the year round.

A prophet of doom in the tenth century could predict 'the fish of the great seas will be sold to the foreigners as soon as they have been brought to land; it will be a sign of evil kingship' – was he referring to the E.E.C. fishing regulations by any chance? In any event, a barrel of salt herrings and dried stockfish hanging from the rafters alongside the flitch of bacon were to be found in almost every farmhouse. And the poor used seaweed to garnish their potatoes. There would often be an eel from the Shannon, too – it teemed with them, just as the streams and lakes did with trout, roach, rudd, pike, bream, carp, smelt, eels and perch. Perch in fact were rated so low that they are still killed off to keep down their numbers, a fact recorded and bewailed by the Irish poet Desmond Egan in his poem, 'Perch'.

Common and worthless in the common opinion
They skit in gangs, dumpy, flashing their ink-red
For the baits of only-youngsters,
– To be secretly tossed, bent now, gaping
Out to the dog. As often as not?
Electrocuted, netted, dumped in shovelfuls
To make room for edible trout. . . Poor perch.

Salmon, on the other hand, were king. Usually, they were baked and grilled, basted with honey and hazelnuts – but whatever the recipe, the salmon was treated with reverence and awe. The High King of Ireland, Cormac Mac Airt, allegedly met his end by choking on a salmon bone – a death fit for a king! Because of its special position, salmon was prepared with almost ritualistic care, its proper presentation demanding three herbs: watercress, marshwort and seaweed.

Orchards and gardens have always been important in Ireland – less so than the salmon, no doubt, but very important all the same. Perhaps the generosity of our soft climate to gardeners has something to do with it – as witnessed by Sir Samuel Ferguson in the nineteenth century.

Large and profitable are the stacks upon the ground
Uileachan Dubh O
The butter and the cream do wondrous well
Uileachan Dubh O
The cresses on the waters and the sorrels are on hand
And the cuckoo's calling daily his note of music bland.

Oats, wheat, barley and rye abounded; also did and still do sorrel, parsnips, carrots, leeks and wild garlic. Even such exotica as salsify and Jerusalem artichokes arrived early on.

Queen Elizabeth's ill-starred favourite, Sir Walter Raleigh, is credited with having brought the potato to Ireland around 1587. Ideally suited to the climate, it soon became the staple diet of the Irish people, an increasing number of whom were living in the poverty of a conquered race. This unquestioning acceptance of the potato by the Irish shocked their contemporaries. In 1665, the court of Besançon in France forbade the cultivation of the potato because of the danger of leprosy. In 1733, a commentator notes with unease the beginning of potato cultivation in Scotland, 'for', he writes, 'no reader of Shakespeare needs to be told that some of the more uncontrollable passions of human nature were supposed to be favoured by its use.' Even in 1792, a critic from France could write of potatoes that they were 'an article of human food which ninety nine hundredths of the human species will not touch.' Yet, in Ireland, the potato was fast growing in popularity. Copland, writing around the time of the Famine, records his amazement at the situation: 'That the potato will, alone, sustain life in full vigour is proved by the Irish peasantry . . . who do not taste animal foods or wheaten bread half a dozen times a year . . . yet a finer body of men are not to be found in any country in Europe.'

But around the same time a Frenchman, de Joannes, sounds more apprehensive on the same subject: 'Its vast productiveness has multiplied potatoes in Ireland so as to form the basis of subsistence of the entire country. That is an evil for a social condition where each family, or nearly each individual, has his field, which furnishes his immediate nutriment without any necessity for marketing, without the assistance of the miller or the baker, without occasion to demand assistance from his neighbours, that society is deficient in the element most necessary to the progress of civilisation.'

An old man, according to tradition, would advise a shy youth at the dinner-table after the threshing: 'Be eating one potato, peeling a second, have a third in your fist and your eye on the fourth.' A lover sings with zest of his beloved whom he met 'in the garden where the praties grow'. Surely there was truth in the notion about the potato that

> The blessed fruit which grows at the root
> Is the real gold of Ireland.

Pratie-cakes (or potato-cakes), Boxty, Stampy, Champ, Nettle, Pea and Chive Champ, Colcannon and Parley all featured potatoes. There seemed as many different variations in potato recipes as there were mothers to cook for the family. An Irishman's appetite has always been worthy of respect. Many a God-fearing farmer thought nothing of eating a stone (6.4 kg) of potatoes at a meal. The man of the house normally undertook to mash the potatoes in an enormous wooden tub with a specially constructed wooden pestle, the beetle.

> Did you ever eat Colcannon when 'twas made with yellow cream
> And the kale and praties blended like the picture in a dream?
> Did you ever take a forkful and dip it in the lake
> Of heather-flavoured butter that your Mother used to make?
> Oh you did; yes you did. So did he and so did I.
> And the more I think about it, sure the more I want to cry
> O God be with the happy times when troubles we had not
> And our Mother made Colcannon in the three legged pot.

In the middle of the nineteenth century – culminating in Black '47 – plague and death swept the land. The potato had been blighted, and a blight fell on the people who were so dependent on it.

Traditionally, vegetables were boiled in meat stocks or fried in bacon fat. Cabbage boiled in water alone was frowned upon. It was referred to as 'bare-footed cabbage' – *cabáiste cosnochtaithe*. A bacon bone or a few chippings from the home-cured side of bacon still makes all the difference to traditional Irish vegetables. Horseradish was much appreciated, even to the extent of being called monk's whiskey – *uisce beatha na mbráthar*. It was usually served with beef and fish. Soups featured too. St Columba lived on Nettle Brotchan while an old Irish document tells us that Esau sold his birthright to Jacob for a *craibeachán* – a broth of meat and vegetables! Butter was another staple of the Irish diet. According to the old proverb, butter was the unction of the heart.

Naturally the story of Irish food has not changed very much, although it is probably true to say that Irish people are becoming more adventurous with food and that Irish chefs have begun to earn an international reputation for our cuisine. Irish food is certainly food for gods and food for saints. For writers, too, needless to remark. In ancient Ireland, the king and the poet were entitled to share the choicest morsels of any beast. Dean Swift (author of *Gulliver's Travels*) was very fond of Dublin Coddle and Spiced Beef and he liked to warm himself up on a winter's night with a good glass of steaming hot Bishop. James Joyce, Sean O'Casey and Brendan Behan all shared a liking for Irish sausages or 'sasiges' as O'Casey's characters called them. When Joyce was living in Paris, his friends knew that all the culinary delights of the French capital were as nothing to him compared with a pound of Findlater's sausages, which he often had sent over. W.B. Yeats was no different, at least in this. Awarded the Nobel Prize, he could think of no more fitting celebration than to head out with 'the boys' for a hearty supper of sausages. The meat content of Irish sausages is exceptionally high: no doubt this, plus the traditional know-how, has contributed to ensuring the fame of true Irish sausages. (Many butchers still make their own, a few times a week.)

As an undergraduate in Trinity College, Samuel Beckett's diet was based on a daily dinner of scrambled eggs, varied only when he had visitors, by switching to an omelet. I have included a special recipe in honour of this great and modest man: Bananas à la Krapp.

All that said, we must still wonder whether the most extraordinary thing about the Irish and their food is their reticence in talking about the matter at all. The Frenchmen, Gault and Millau, put this singular attitude down to a form of psychosis. A kind of Jansenism? An otherworldliness that baulks at the purely physical? Perhaps; perhaps not. We have had the first word from Patrick Kavanagh so why not the last word – and its insight – from him also.

You're far too great a genius to
Talk of steak and onions or a stew.

SOUPS

From the faraway times that invented Brotchan Roy and Grunt soup right up to the present day, soups – good, rich, substantial ''atin' and drinkin' ' soups – have played a very important part in the Irish diet, as in the diet of our Scottish neighbours. Earlier forms of broth contained no meat, unless maybe a piece of lard. Oatmeal and homegrown vegetables, especially leeks, salsify and cresses were popular. St Columba, we are told, lived the best years of his life on Nettle Soup.

When the Great Famine decimated the countryside, the French chef, Alexis Soyer, left his kitchens in the Reform Club in London to help with his specially-devised soups. His brief was 'to produce the greatest amount of food at a minimum cost and with maximum nutrition'. He received the title Head Cook of all Ireland. His ideas caught on like wild-fire, and soup kitchens sprang up everywhere to eke out the resources of the famine- and plague-stricken population. Poor Soyer got little or no thanks for his bright idea, as we see from this parody of the Three Witches in *Macbeth*, taken from the *Nation*, a patriotic newspaper of the time.

First Witch: Round about the boiler go,
                  In twice fifty gallons throw,
                  Watch that in the noisome tank
                  Mossed with verdure rich and rank.
Second Witch: Shin of beef from skinny cow
                  In the boiler then you'll throw;
                  Onion sliced, and turnip top,
                  Crumb of bread and cabbage chop.
Third Witch: Scale of cod-fish, spider's tongue,
                  Tom-tits' gizzards, heads and lungs
                  Of a famished French-fed frog,
                  Root of pratie digged in bog.

For a variety of reasons, hysteria set in and poor Soyer fled secretly

from the country, in fear of being lynched. But his idea lived on in the 'soup runs' which the gentry continued to organise for the starving peasantry. Word went round that they were proselytizing soups and a new word entered the language, the 'souper', the person who in order to get soup abandons his religion, Catholicism, and turns Protestant. A 'souper' was easily recognized: he was a Protestant who bore a Catholic surname.

Irish soups tend to be rich and hearty – a meal in themselves. Nowadays, with shredders, liquidizers and blenders, soup-making should undergo a renaissance.

· LEEK AND MUSSEL SOUP.

Leek and Mussel Soup

2.4 litres (4 pints) mussels
300 ml (½ pint) cider
2 leeks, finely chopped
1 shallot, finely chopped
6 black peppercorns, crushed
3 sprigs of fennel
4 tablespoons parsley
900 ml (1½ pints) fish stock
50 g (2 oz) butter
50 g (2 oz) flour
2 egg yolks
150 ml (¼ pint) cream

Clean and prepare the mussels. Any even slightly open which do not snap shut when sharply tapped should be discarded. Watch out for shells filled with mud or sand – even one such shell is enough to ruin a dish. Put cider, finely chopped leeks, shallot, pepper and herbs in pan. Cover. Turn up the heat and steam the mussels for a minute or two until the mussels open. Remove from the heat. Empty the mussels and their juices from shells into the pan. Keep the mussels warm. Add the fish stock to the pan juices. Blend the flour and butter together and stir into the simmering stock. Continue simmering for about 10 minutes until the soup thickens and the flour is well cooked. Remove from the heat. Add the egg yolks, beaten up with the cream. Stir well into the soup. Return to the heat and allow to simmer very gently for a few moments only. On no account allow to boil at this stage. Test for seasoning with salt and pepper. Serve 5–6 mussels as a garnish to each bowl of soup. *Serves 4–6.*

Brotchan Roy

50 g (2 oz) butter
50 g (2 oz) oatmeal
900 ml (1½ pints) stock or water
300 ml (½ pint) milk
225 g (½ lb) shredded leeks
pepper and salt
pinch of mace
parsley

Brotchan is an old Gaelic word meaning broth.

**Melt the butter and add the oatmeal. Fry gently until crisp and toasted. Stir in the stock or water, and the milk. Add the leeks and seasoning and bring to the boil. Simmer gently for ½–1 hour. Just before serving, sprinkle with parsley.
    Serve with steaming hot soda bread** *Serves 4.*

Nettle Brotchan

50 g (2 oz) butter
50 g (2 oz) oatmeal
900 ml (1½ pints) stock or water
300 ml (½ pint) milk
450 g (1 lb) shredded nettles
1 onion, peeled and chopped
salt, pepper and a little mace
chopped parsley

Down by the glenside I met an old woman;
A-plucking young nettles, she ne'er saw me comin',
I listened a while to the song she was hummin' –
'Glory-o, glory-o to the bould Fenian Men.'

Young, tender spring nettle shoots seemingly work wonders, cleansing and purifying the blood after the strain of winter. The Irish believed that 'at least three dinners of nettles are essential in April and May'.

Nettle was also useful as an aphrodisiac and love philtres were mixed from it. Nettles also provided a powerful medicine for all sores, swellings, and especially for shingles.

Melt the butter in a pan and gently fry the oatmeal until crisp and toasted. Stir in the stock or water and the milk. Add the shredded nettles and chopped onion. Season and bring to the boil. Lower the heat and simmer gently for $\frac{1}{4}-\frac{1}{2}$ hour. Liquidize, if liked, and serve sprinkled with parsley. *Serves 4–6.*

Limpet and Clam Soup

10 limpets
4 clams
4 mussels
300 ml ($\frac{1}{2}$ pint) cider
juice of one lemon
1 small leek or onion, finely
  chopped
1 potato, peeled and chopped
a few threads of saffron
150 ml ($\frac{1}{4}$ pint) cream
sea-salt and freshly ground pepper
1 tablespoon each parsley and
  chives, finely chopped

Put scrubbed shellfish in a large pan with 600 ml (1 pint) water, the cider, lemon juice, leek or onion, potato and saffron. Bring to the boil. Allow to simmer for a few minutes. Remove mussels and clams a few minutes after they open and keep warm. Limpets are usually quite tough and need long, slow cooking so continue to cook gently for $\frac{1}{2}-\frac{3}{4}$ hour until the liquid is reduced by about one-third. Stir cream into the soup. Check the seasoning. Distribute the shellfish (chop the larger ones in two or three pieces) in soup bowls. Sprinkle with chopped parsley and chives.

Serve with home-made brown bread and butter. *Serves 4.*

Grunt Soup

$\frac{1}{2}$ onion, peeled and finely chopped
25 g (1 oz) butter
1 small carrot, finely diced
450 g (1 lb) grunt or young perch
600 ml (1 pint) water
salt and pepper
15 g (1 tablespoon) cornflour
150 ml ($\frac{1}{4}$ pint) cream

This traditional soup comes from the Lough Neagh region in the north of Ireland. *Grunt* are the young of perch – which abound in every lake in Ireland. They are so full of little bones that they are not considered suitable for frying.

Soften the onion in the butter in a heavy saucepan without letting it brown. Add the carrot and cook gently for a few minutes. Rinse the grunt in lots of fresh water and add it to the pan with the water, salt and pepper. Bring to the boil, lower the heat and simmer gently for $\frac{1}{4}-\frac{1}{2}$ hour. Lift out the fish and carefully remove as much flesh as possible from them. Return the fish flesh to the soup. Blend the

cornflour with a little water and use to thicken the soup. Correct the seasoning and stir in the cream. *Serves 4.*

Fish Soup

450 g (1 lb) fishbones, heads,
    trimmings etc.
small onion stuck with two cloves
bay leaf
salt and black peppercorns
a few parsley sprigs
25 g (1 oz) butter
25 g (1 oz) flour
300 ml ($\frac{1}{2}$ pint) milk
2 tablespoons yogurt
juice of $\frac{1}{2}$ lemon

Make a good rich stock by covering the fish bones and other trimmings with cold water. Add onion, bay leaf, salt and peppercorns and some of the parsley. Bring to the boil, then simmer for $\frac{1}{2}$ hour. Strain. Melt the butter in a saucepan and stir in the flour. Cook gently for a few minutes. Gradually add about 600 ml (1 pint) of stock and the milk. Simmer again for a few minutes. Add the yogurt and lemon juice. Season well. Sprinkle with the rest of the chopped parsley and serve. *Serves 4.*

Mixed Fish Soup

50 g (2 oz) butter or lard
2 cloves garlic, chopped
4 shallots, chopped
450 g (1 lb) tomatoes
1.8 litres (3 pints) boiling water
1 small whiting
1 cod's head
100 g (4 oz) skate
sole or plaice bones, if available
    from fishmonger
pinch of saffron or 1 teaspoon
    turmeric
salt, red and black pepper
150 ml ($\frac{1}{4}$ pint) dry cider
chopped parsley to garnish

Heat the butter or lard in a pan. Add chopped garlic and shallots, then the skinned and chopped tomatoes. Mash with a wooden spoon and continue cooking until soft and mushy. Pour in the water and cider. Add the fish and cook gently for $\frac{1}{2}$ hour. Remove head and skin. Add saffron, salt and pepper. Continue cooking until the fish has disintegrated. Sieve to remove bones. Serve piping hot and garnished with chopped parsley. *Serves 6.*

Ennis Cockle Soup

2 dozen large cockles
2 potatoes, peeled and chopped
1 celery stalk, sliced
2 leeks, washed and sliced
1 bay leaf
600 ml (1 pint) water
600 ml (1 pint) milk
salt and pepper

'Bringing cockles to Ennis' is the Irish equivalent of bringing coals to Newcastle. Cockles were extremely plentiful along the Clare coast. This was a lucky thing for Ennis since cockles in Ancient Ireland were regarded as food fit for Kings!

Prepare cockles by leaving overnight in a bucket of clean fresh water – this not only cleans them but rids them of excess salt. Cook potato, celery, leeks and bay leaf in the milk and water for about 20 minutes. Drop cockles into saucepan, checking

19

each one for soundness. They will quickly open and in a few minutes be cooked. Remove shells and bay leaf. Adjust seasoning. Sprinkle with parsley and serve. *Serves 4–6.*

Mac Dá Thó's Pea Soup

2 crubeens (pig's trotters)
1.2 litres (2 pints) water
6 peppercorns
2 large onions, chopped
225 g (8 oz) dried peas, soaked
    overnight
2 sage leaves
2 stalks of celery, finely chopped
1 tablespoon parsley, finely
    chopped

Mac Dá Thó's pig was served up at a legendary feast in ancient Ireland. The pig was so fat that he had six inches of fat on his snout.

Boil crubeens and peppercorns in the water for 2 or 3 hours. Skim off fat and scum. Add chopped onions, peas, sage and celery and cook for a further 30 minutes. Remove crubeens. Sieve or liquidize soup and serve garnished with parsley. *Serves 4.*

Fresh Garden Pea Soup

900 g (2 lb) garden peas
1 head lettuce, shredded
a few scallions or spring onions,
    chopped
600 ml (1 pint) water
pinch of sugar
salt
50 g (2oz) butter
finely chopped mint
300 ml (½ pint) cream (optional)

Unless the peas are very old and stringy use pods and all. Put all the ingredients, except for the butter and mint, in a casserole together and cook until tender. Sieve to remove fibres and then liquidize. Add a little more water or stock to bring the soup to the right consistency. Check taste for saltiness. Just before serving add the butter and a little finely chopped mint.
    To add a touch of luxury, stir in about 300 ml (½ pint) cream at the last moment. *Serves 4.*

St John's Day Soup (Salmon Head Soup)

1 salmon head
900 ml (1½ pints) fish stock
25 g (1 oz) butter
25 g (1 oz) flour
300 ml (½ pint) milk
salt and black pepper
chopped parsley

Traditionally St John's Day, in Coleraine and along the shores of Lough Neagh in Northern Ireland, was a day of great feasting on Salmon. It was always accompanied by new potatoes and washed down with lots of Bushmill's best Irish Whiskey.

Poach the salmon head in stock for about 10 minutes. Take head out and remove all flesh. Flake and set aside. Return head to pan and boil until the liquid is reduced by about ⅓. Blend the butter,

flour and milk together. Add to stock. Bring to the boil and cook well for 5 minutes. Remove head. Add flaked salmon and simmer for a few moments. Season and serve garnished with chopped parsley. *Serves 4–6.*

Cabbage Soup

225 g (8 oz) lean bacon, diced
1.8 litres (3 pints) water
6 black peppercorns
450 g (1 lb) cabbage, shredded
1 small turnip, diced
2 carrots, diced
3 – 4 potatoes, diced
1 bay leaf
2 tablespoons parsley, chopped

Cabbage seems to have been cultivated first by the Celts. The words 'cabbage' and 'kale' seem to come from the Celtic words '*cab*' and '*cál*'. The word '*cál*' is also found in Colcannon, the traditional Irish dish made up of a mixture of potatoes and, ideally, kale.

Bring bacon to the boil in the water with peppercorns and cook for about ½ hour. Add the prepared vegetables and the bay leaf to the boiling stock. Season. Simmer for about 10–15 minutes more until the vegetables are tender. Sprinkle with parsley and serve very hot. *Serves 6.*

Broad Bean Soup

1 ham bone, crubeen (pig's trotter) or stock cube
1 large onion
50 g (2 oz) butter
25 g (1 oz) flour
225 g (8 oz) broad beans, fresh or frozen
1 level teaspoon dried oregano, or sprig of rosemary
dash of lemon juice
salt and freshly ground pepper

Make stock by simmering ham bone or crubeen in 900 ml (1½ pints) water for an hour or so, or make it up using the stock cube. Fry onion and garlic in butter until soft but not coloured. Stir in flour and cook for a few minutes before adding the stock. Add the broad beans and the oregano, lemon juice, salt and pepper. Simmer, covered, until the beans are tender. Blend or sieve, adding water if necessary, to obtain a thin creamy consistency. *Serves 4.*

Fresh Lettuce Soup

2 young lettuces
4 scallions or spring onions
50 g (2 oz) butter
600 ml (1 pint) chicken stock
300 ml (½ pint) milk
1 bay leaf
pinch of nutmeg
salt and pepper
4 tablespoons cream
chopped parsley

Remove hard stalks and any discoloured outer leaves from the lettuces. Shred finely. Trim roots from scallions and wash thoroughly. Slice thinly. Melt butter in pan and cook scallions and lettuce gently for about 15 minutes. Add stock and milk, also the bay leaf. Bring to the boil, then leave to simmer for about 30 minutes. Add nutmeg, salt and pepper to taste. Sieve. Add cream and garnish with parsley just before serving. *Serves 3–4.*

21

Brosna Watercress Soup

50 g (2 oz) butter or lard
1 onion, peeled and chopped
25 g (1 oz) flour
600 ml (1 pint) chicken stock
2 potatoes, peeled and chopped
3 bunches of watercress
sea-salt and freshly ground pepper
5 tablespoons cream

'If you don't get the meat, the soup is worth a lot.' (Irish proverb)

Melt butter or lard in a heavy-bottomed pan and cook the onion until soft but not browned. Stir in the flour and cook gently for two minutes. Gradually stir in the stock. Add potatoes. Bring to the boil and cook for a few minutes. Wash watercress thoroughly under lots of running water. Chop finely and add to the soup. Cook for about 5 minutes. Liquidize or rub the mixture through the sieve. Re-heat, and correct seasoning. Stir in cream. Garnish with a few leaves of watercress. *Serves 3–4.*

Fish and Vegetable Broth

50 g (2 oz) streaky rashers
1 medium onion, peeled and
    chopped
100 g (4 oz) potatoes, peeled and
    chopped
½ stick celery, chopped
1 carrot, scraped and chopped
1.2 litres (2 pints) fish stock or
    water
sprigs of parsley and fennel
450 g (1 lb) white fish
salt and pepper
finely chopped parsley

Chop the rashers and fry them for a few minutes in their own fat. Add chopped onion and fry until transparent but not brown. Cook the prepared potatoes, celery, and carrot for a few minutes with the rashers and onions. Add the fish stock or water, the parsley and fennel and simmer gently for about 20 minutes before adding all the fish. Reduce heat and poach fish gently for 5–6 minutes. Lift fish from pan and remove skin and bones. Return the fish to the pan and boil the soup until it reduces by about ¼. By now, the fish and vegetables will have more or less disintegrated. With a wooden spoon, pound the debris of fish and vegetables. If liked, strain through a sieve, or liquidize. Adjust the seasoning with salt and pepper. Add a generous squeeze of lemon juice. Sprinkle with finely chopped parsley and serve. *Serves 4.*

Jerusalem Artichoke Soup

450 g (1 lb) Jerusalem Artichokes
50 g (2 oz) butter
900 ml (1½ pints) vegetable stock
salt and freshly ground pepper
pinch of sugar

Jerusalem Artichokes have nothing to do with either Jerusalem or Artichokes! The Jerusalem part of the name is a corruption of the Italian word *girasole* meaning a sunflower (the tuber belongs, in fact, to the sunflower family). Someone then called it an artichoke because they thought the taste vaguely resembled that of the artichoke. It came to Ireland around the same time as the potato – or maybe a little

· JERUSALEM
ARTICHOKE
SOUP ·

earlier. It was first regarded as manna from Heaven because it was extraordinarily prolific and very filling – just the thing to feed the teeming poor. Then the potato caught on, and the Jerusalem Artichoke fell somewhat from favour.

The biggest problem is peeling this knobbledy, wart-covered vegetable. But it is worth persevering for this truly is a delicious soup.
     Scrub the tubers thoroughly and parboil for 20 – 25 minutes in salted water. Drain and cool. The skins will now pull off quite easily and the sweet nutty taste of the artichokes is retained better than if they had been peeled beforehand. Chop the artichokes and soften in a pan with the butter – taking care not to let them brown. Add the salt, pepper, and sugar, then the stock, and simmer for about ½ hour until really soft. Sieve. *Serves 4.*

Traditional Spinach and Oatmeal Soup

25 g (1 oz) butter
50 g (2 oz) oatmeal
1.2 litres (2 pints) stock
175 g (6 oz) potatoes, peeled and
     diced
mace, salt and pepper
225 g (8 oz) spinach, cooked
chives
1 tablespoon cream

Melt butter and gently fry the oatmeal until crisp. Add stock and diced potatoes with the seasoning. Bring to the boil and simmer for ½–¾ hour, adding spinach and chives for the last five minutes of cooking. Sieve. Re-heat and stir in the cream. *Serves 4.*

Carrot Soup

1.2 litres (2 pints) chicken stock
450 g (1 lb) carrots
1 onion
50 g (2 oz) butter
salt
pinch of sugar
1 medium potato, peeled and
     finely chopped

Make up stock, using a stock cube if necessary. Scrape and thinly slice the carrots and onion. Put in a pan with the butter and cook for a few minutes. Add salt and sugar. Add stock and finely chopped potato. Simmer until really soft. Sieve or liquidize. If necessary, dilute with a little more water, or cream if available. *Serves 4–6.*

Leek Soup

225 g (8 oz) leeks
500 g (1 lb) potatoes
900 ml (1½ pints) water
salt and pepper

If leekes you like, but their smell dis-leeke
Eat onyons and you shall not smell the leek.
If you of onyons would the scent expel
Eat garlicke, that shall drown the onyon's smell.

23

600 ml (1 pint) milk
50 g (2 oz) butter

Split the leeks and wash them thoroughly in lots of running water to remove all clay. Then chop them. Peel and chop potatoes. Put vegetables in a pan with the cold water, salt and pepper and simmer gently for about 1 hour. Sieve. Add the milk and reheat. Serve in soup bowls with a knob of butter in each. *Serves 4–6.*

Sorrel Soup

450 g (1 lb) potatoes, peeled and chopped
225 g (8 oz) sorrel, stalks removed
25 g (1 oz) butter
salt
4 soupspoons fresh cream

Sorrel was probably widely cultivated in Ireland from the fifteenth century.

Boil the potatoes in 1.2 litres (2 pints) salty water until soft. Meanwhile, wash the sorrel leaves, chop and soften them over a low heat in a little butter for about 5 minutes. Add to the potatoes, with some salt, and continue cooking for another 15 minutes. Sieve or liquidize the soup. Stir in the cream and serve. *Serves 4.*

Tomato Soup

25 g (1 oz) butter
50 g (2 oz) streaky bacon, chopped
1 onion, chopped
1 small carrot, chopped
450 g (1 lb) tomatoes, peeled and chopped
1 potato, chopped
½ bay leaf
1 clove garlic
sprig of parsley
pinch of basil or oregano
1.2 litres (2 pints) water

Melt the butter and add the bacon, chopped onion and carrot together to the pan. Brown lightly. Plunge tomatoes into boiling water for a few seconds to make them easier to peel. Add peeled, chopped tomatoes and potatoes, crushed garlic and herbs to the pan. Simmer very gently until soft and mushy and the flavours have blended. Sieve. Add the water to purée and continue cooking for another 10–15 minutes. *Serves 4.*

.TOMATO SOUP.

FISh

Ireland is a small island boasting 2,000 miles of coastline warmed by the Gulf Stream and teeming with many kinds of fish. Freshwater fish also abound in the rich and unpolluted lakes, rivers and streams which plough the limestone interior of the country. We have, and always have had, fish in abundance, but surprisingly the Irish attitude to fish has always been ambivalent. Perhaps the early Celtic taboo on fish-eating lay at the root of this: the elements – including water – were worshipped, hence fish-eating was commonly regarded as a profanity.

Early on, the salmon, our only large native fish, escaped from this taboo to become highly prized. Stories of this delicious fish weave through the story of Ireland. It was the food of kings and of lovers. King Dagda and Fionn MacCuil enjoyed it – indeed, Fionn owed his legendary wisdom to his being the first to taste the famous Salmon of Knowledge. Maybe another story is nearer to the truth. It seems that Fionn astounded his followers one day by luring a magnificent salmon from the stream using nothing but a piece of cord and a rowan berry. Word spread – and with it, Fionn's reputation for wisdom. The Red Branch lovers, Deirdre and Naoise from Armagh, before their tragic fate overtook them, feasted on salmon. In the other end of the country, down in Co. Kerry, Diarmuid O Duibhne, eloping with the King of Ireland's betrothed, and hotly pursued by a very angry and powerful King, still found time to catch and enjoy a salmon poached from the river Leane. Not surprisingly, salmon is still a traditional festive dish for Christmas in Kerry.

Irish mythology can also explain how the salmon got his gorgeous spots. Nine hazel trees – and the hazel in those days was a sacred tree, its wood being used to make wands – grew at the head of the Irish rivers. In autumn, the hazelnuts fell into the water and on to the salmon, marking them with their distinctive spots.

As might be expected, given the salmon's popularity, salmon weirs, where the fish could be caught easily, sprang up all over the country. After the Battle of Clontarf in 1014, when Brian Boru,

Emperor of the Irish, defeated the invading Danes, the great chief's grandson Turloch was found dead, impaled on one of the stakes of the Tolka salmon weir. Again, Leixlip on the Liffey gets its name from the salmon who traditionally leaped in the Liffey waterfall: *leix* comes from a Norse word *lax*, meaning salmon. A French visitor to Ireland in 1672 was impressed to find salmon for sale at 3 pence but as late as 1962, there were so many salmon on the market that fish-and-chip shops found it as cheap to serve salmon as the more traditional whiting, ray or cod.

The arrival of Christianity in the fifth century, with its emphasis on abstinence from meat, gave a boost to fish consumption. Not only were the usual fish eaten, but Adamnan in his Life of that valiant Irishman St Columba tells us how the Irish monks in Iona held the flesh of seals in high esteem. Herrings became a part of life. They were eaten fresh in summer, fried in oatmeal and dripping; for winter, they were salted or dried. A huge barrel of salted herrings was part of the furniture in every farmhouse kitchen. The salted herring with maybe a bit of *sliúcháin* (sloke) or *duilisc* (dulse) was often the only garnish for the potatoes.

There are plenty of shellfish around our coast. The native mussel (*Mytilus edulis*) can be found just about everywhere waiting to be gathered. Nowadays, more and more mussels are being farmed. Surprisingly, mussel-farming was invented by an Irishman. In 1235, a native with the unlikely name of Walton and two companions were bringing a shipload of finest Irish lamb to France when they were caught in a storm and shipwrecked. Walton alone survived and managed to clamber ashore at Escande in the Bay of Aiguillon. Starving and destitute, he wandered along the shore, noticing the thousands of mussels clinging to the harbour stakes. They seemed to grow faster and fatter than the other wild variety. This observation, coupled with the prevalent need for mussels, led him to invent his farming technique. To this day, this method, now called the *bouchot* method, is the most commonly used in France. In Ireland a variation is favoured, using ropes and flat rafts. Mussel seed is dredged up from the overcrowded Irish Sea and transferred for fattening to more favoured spots like Killary Harbour, Cromane or Wexford – just as beef is transferred from the hungry grass of Roscommon to the rich plains of Meath for finishing.

The native oyster (*Ostrea edulis*) has a really rich flavour and is much sought after by gourmets. The only problem is that we can't get enough oysters and also – since they spawn in summer – cannot eat them in a month without an 'r', that is, from May until August. Relatively slow-growing, they take from three to five years to reach maturity. They are then usually about 7.6 cms (3 inches) in diameter, and at their best served up, freshly opened and chilled, on a bed of crushed ice and lemon wedges, garnished with seaweed.

The great oyster eaters of Galway like to serve their oysters in the flat shell – which seems a terrible waste since in this way the subtly flavoured juices of the oyster are lost. Elsewhere the oyster is served in the rounded shell. In recent years, the Pacific oyster (*Crassostrea gigas*) has been introduced. With a nice, frilly, pear-shaped shell, this oyster isn't as well flavoured as the native variety, but it grows quickly and is ready for the table in a year or two. Another advantage of the Pacific oyster is that it is available for consumption all the year round – because of the coolness of Irish waters, it doesn't spawn here, unless in hatcheries. Normally it is cheaper to buy and much larger than the native, but lacks the latter's flavour and is perhaps best prepared cooked.

Lobster, crab, crayfish and scallops abound side by side with cockles, periwinkles, clams, limpets and razor fish. Many of these varieties can be found by an adventurous cook at lowtide on the miles of unpolluted beaches. Alexis Soyer, who was conferred with the title of Head Cook of Ireland, was surprised to see people in the West cooking cockles in their shells over the turf fires and eating them with oatcakes. Had he gone to Inchmore, a tiny island in the Shannon's Lough Ree, he might have seen the islanders storing freshly caught eels alive in a small pool out of which they were fished at dinner-times. An old-world variation on the fish-tank found today in classy restaurants!

The rivers and lakes are still full of salmon, trout and eels – but it seems to take skill and experience to catch them. Pike, shad, mullet, carp, roach, brea, rudd and tench – coarse fish – can be found nearly everywhere. The limestone lakes in the centre of the country (Loughs Lene, Sheelin and Derravaragh, etc.) teem with freshwater crayfish. Though slightly smaller than the American crayfish (introduced to many Continental waters), they are just as tasty.

. D V B L I N
L A W Y E R .

Oysters with Guinness

Everybody agrees that oysters, particularly the excellent native variety, are best eaten raw, in their natural state, fresh from the shell with, if you like, the merest trickle of lemon juice. In Ireland, generations of gourmets have washed down their oysters with lots of creamy Guinness beer.

Store the oysters in the vegetable compartment of the fridge, and open them only minutes before serving. To open, grasp the oyster, wrapped in a cloth, in the palm of one hand. Insert a sharp knife into the hinge of the shell. Jack upwards, and with luck, the oyster will open. If you cannot manage that, try using a pair of pliers to nip a piece out of the shell, opposite the hinge. The shell should then open easily. Finally, if those methods defeat you, simply put the oysters under a really hot grill for a few seconds until they start opening spontaneously.

Take care not to spill the oyster juices in the shell. They can be consumed with the oyster, or kept and added to soups, stews, etc.

Serve them on a bed of ice with lemon wedges, and maybe garnished with a few sprays of seaweed. With lots of freshly baked, crusty brown bread, you have a meal to remember.

Marinated Oysters

4 dozen oysters
8 shallots, peeled and finely
   chopped
bunch of fresh herbs: parsley,
   chives and tarragon, all finely
   chopped
salt and pepper
3 soupspoons olive oil
1 lemon

Open the oysters and remove them from their shells without their juices. Place them in a serving dish, sprinkle the chopped herbs and shallots over them. Add salt and pepper to taste. Squeeze the juice from the lemon, mix with the olive oil (or any good-quality oil) and pour over the oysters, shallots and herbs. Marinate in the refrigerator for at least 1 hour before serving. *Serves 4.*

Fried Oysters

20 oysters
100 g (4 oz) fine breadcrumbs
salt and pepper
parsley, finely chopped
1 egg, beaten
1 tablespoon milk

'An oyster may be crossed in love.'
(Richard Brinsley Sheridan)

Open the oysters, carefully collecting their juices. Put them in a saucepan and parboil them in their own juices. Strain and dry in a clean cloth. Coat

28

To garnish
1 bunch of watercress

with fine breadcrumbs. Beat the egg and then dilute with the tablespoon of milk. Season well with salt and pepper and a little very finely chopped parsley. Dip the oysters in the egg mixture and then coat again with breadcrumbs.

Meanwhile, heat the fat to between 350°F and 365°F (Gas 4, 180°C). Fry the oysters for 3–4 minutes in the hot fat until golden brown. Drain on kitchen paper and serve garnished with watercress. *Serves 4.*

Stuffed Grilled Oysters

225 g (8 oz) butter
2 cloves garlic, peeled and crushed
½ onion, peeled and finely chopped
1 tablespoon parsley, finely
    chopped
salt and pepper
100 g (4 oz) grated Irish Cheddar
    cheese
4 dozen oysters
3 tablespoons browned
    breadcrumbs

Cream the butter, crushed garlic, onion and parsley together. Add salt and pepper to taste. Open the oysters and pour off the liquid. Cover the oysters in their shells with the flavoured butter. Sprinkle with a mixture of grated Cheddar and breadcrumbs. Arrange the oysters in their shells on a dish, making sure they don't spill over. Cook in a moderate oven (350°F, 180°C, Gas 4) for 20–25 minutes. *Serves 4.*

Lobster with Cream and Irish Whiskey

1 lobster, weighing about 1 kg (2
    lb), cooked
25 g (1 oz) butter
70 ml (4 tablespoons) Irish
    Whiskey
300 ml (½ pint) white sauce,
    blending 13 g (½ oz) flour and 13
    g (½ oz) butter with 300 ml (1
    pint) milk
150 ml (¼ pint) double cream

Remove and cut up the flesh of the cooked lobster. Toss in the hot butter for 1 minute. Heat the whiskey, set alight and pour over the lobster pieces. When the flames die down, pour in enough cream to coat the lobster and then fold in the white sauce made by blending the flour, butter and milk. If liked, the lobster half-shells can be filled with this mixture. *Serves 2.*

Dublin Lawyer

1 medium-sized lobster
150 ml (¼ pint) cream
50 g (2 oz) butter
4 tablespoons Irish Whiskey
salt and pepper

This traditional gourmet dish is Ireland's version of France's *homard à la crème*.

This dish is better flavoured if made with raw lobster. Your fishmonger will kill and slice a live lobster down the centre lengthwise. Remove the little grit bag near the head. Remove also the soft greenish coral and keep. Break and remove the flesh from the claws. Remove the flesh also from the tail and head. Cut into chunks.

Heat the butter in a pan taking care not to let it brown. Cook the raw lobster, including the coral in the butter for a few minutes. Season to taste.

Warm the whiskey. Pour over the lobster and flame it. Stir in the cream and let it heat through gently – on no account allow to boil.

Serve the mixture piled into the lobster shells, or arrange the lobster shells side by side on the serving dish with the lobster mixture piled into the centre. *Serves 2.*

Dressed Lobster

1 lobster, weighing about 1 kg (2 lb)

For the dressing
4 tablespoons olive oil
1 tablespoon Dijon mustard
parsley, tarragon and chives, finely chopped
1 onion, peeled and finely chopped
12 drops soya sauce
freshly ground white pepper
small glass Pernod or pastis.

The sauce suggested was invented by Alexandre Dumas and is in his *Grand Dictionnaire de Cuisine*. Its spicy lightness seems to go much better with the rich lobster meat than the traditional mayonnaise.

Cook the lobster by plunging it into a large saucepan of boiling salted water – sea-water is ideal. (The RSPCA recommend that the unfortunate creature should be plunged into cool water and the water boiled gradually in a lidded pot.) Simmer for 25 minutes, remove from water and allow to cool. When cool, remove the flesh from the body and having removed the dark intestinal thread, dice the meat from the tail. Split the claws, remove and dice this meat also. Mix all the ingredients for the sauce together, and fold in the diced lobster. *Serves 3–4.*

Dublin Bay Prawns with Garlic Butter

50 g (2 oz) butter
1 clove garlic
450 g (1 lb) cooked Dublin Bay Prawns, shelled
salt and pepper
a few sprigs of parsley
1 lemon, quartered

For some curious and unclear reason, Dublin Bay Prawns don't belong to the prawn family at all. The specialist recognizes this delicious mouthful as a Norway lobster. To add further to a confused situation, our Dublin Bay Prawns mysteriously become scampi when coated in batter and deep-fried.

Melt the butter in a heavy-bottomed pan. Crush the garlic, add to the butter in the pan and heat gently. Toss the prawns in the pan for just long enough to heat them through. Season with salt and pepper. Serve immediately with lemon wedges and sprigs of fresh parsley. *Serves 4.*

Dublin Bay Prawns with Irish Whiskey

1 large onion, chopped
1 clove of garlic, chopped
50 g (2 oz) butter
1 tablespoon flour
300 ml (½ pint) fish stock
150 ml (¼ pint) double cream
salt and pepper
450 g (1 lb) Dublin Bay Prawns, cooked and shelled
72 ml (4 tablespoons) Irish whiskey

Cook the onion and garlic in about 25 g (1 oz) of butter until soft but not brown. Stir in the flour, then add the fish stock and cream. Simmer for about a half hour or so. Season.

Reheat the Dublin Bay Prawns in the remaining butter. Warm the whiskey. Pour the whiskey over the heated prawns and set alight. Shake the pan a few times so that the flaming whiskey fully flavours all the prawns. When the flames die down, pour the sauce over them. Stir, heat thoroughly and serve immediately. *Serves 4.*

Dublin Bay Prawns in Soured Cream Sauce

50 g (2 oz) butter
3 teaspoons lemon juice
100 g (4 oz) soured cream
2 medium-sized egg yolks
salt and pepper
225 g (8 oz) Dublin Bay Prawns cooked and shelled
paprika
4 slices of toast

Melt the butter in a heavy-bottomed saucepan. Stir in the lemon juice, soured cream and egg yolks. Cook over a very low heat, stirring all the time, until the sauce thickens. Take care that it doesn't boil. Season with salt and pepper. Add the prawns and leave for a few minutes for the prawns to heat through.

To serve, spoon the prawns with the sauce on to the four slices of toast, sprinkle lightly with paprika and serve immediately. *Serves 4.*

Mornington Mussels

1.2 litres (2 pints) mussels
1 bay leaf
½ onion, finely chopped
1 tablespoon salt
25 g (1 oz) butter
25 g (1 oz) flour
300 ml (½ pint) milk
juice of ½ lemon
pepper and salt

Mornington mussels are said to be the best in Western Europe and yet they are available along the quays of Drogheda for half nothing.

Scrub the mussels and check that each one of them is quite fresh. Put them in a pan with the bay leaf and the onion and a little salt. Add 3 tablespoons of cold water. Cover and put on the heat for a few minutes until the shells open. Take the shells from the pan and remove mussels from the shells. Strain the liquor from the pan. Blend the butter and flour together. Add the milk gradually and then stir into the liquor from the mussels. Boil for 4 minutes. Add lemon juice and season. Pour over the mussels and reheat if necessary. Serve with thinly-cut slices of brown bread and butter. *Serves 2.*

Vintage Atlantic Casserole

150 ml (¼ pint) white wine
1 clove of garlic, finely chopped
2 medium onions, peeled and
    finely chopped
225 g (8 oz) salmon
175 g (6 oz) monkfish
4 medium scallops
175 g (6 oz) shelled prawns
8 clams or mussels
black pepper but no salt
300 ml (½ pint) thick white sauce
1 level teaspoon chopped herbs

This dish is a speciality of Gerry and Marie Galvin's restaurant in Kinsale. The dish is built around any four different kinds of fish caught locally – they usually include salmon, monkfish, scallops and prawns, with either mussels or clams in their shells for decoration.

**Bring wine, garlic and chopped onions to the boil in a large saucepan. Add salmon and monkfish and simmer for 10 minutes, adding scallops after 5 minutes and shelled prawns after 8. Prepare the clams or mussels, open them in a covered pan over a high heat, then keep warm until required. Remove the fish from the pan and keep warm. Dilute the thick white sauce with about 150 ml (¼ pint) of the cooking liquid. Serve the fish in a heated earthenware bowl. Pour the sauce over it and decorate with fresh herbs and the clams, mussels or prawns. *Serves 4–6.*

Crab Salad

2 700 g – 900 g (1½ – 2 lb) crabs,
    cooked
100 g (4 oz) celery, diced
4 – 5 small tomatoes, quartered
parsley, chopped

For the dressing
2 tablespoons olive oil
1 tablespoon vinegar
½ teaspoon made mustard
¼ teaspoon salt
¼ teaspoon pepper

To garnish
a few radishes and leaves of lettuce

**Remove the meat from the crabs and cut into neat pieces. Add the celery, tomatoes and some of the parsley. To prepare the dressing, add the seasoning to the oil. Then add the vinegar, a drop at a time, and mix thoroughly with a wooden spoon until it thickens a little. Arrange the crab mixture on a dish on a few leaves of lettuce. Cut the radishes into roses and decorate the dish with them. Pour the dressing over the whole lot. *Serves 4–6.*

Clogherhead Crab Paste

1 large crab
1 teaspoon chives
1 teaspoon grated horseradish
1 tablespoon cream
lemon juice
50 g (2 oz) butter
salt and freshly ground black
    pepper

**Always make sure this most delicious shellfish is live when purchased. Choose the heaviest rather than the largest crab. To cook, plunge into lots of boiling salted water. Boil for 3–4 minutes, then reduce heat and simmer for 20 minutes. When cooked, twist off all legs. Pull or lever top part of shell from lower part. Remove lungs (in the bony part) and the sac (at the top of the big shell). All the rest is edible. If you are lucky enough to get a female crab in summer, as well as with meat she

will be packed with a thick spongy pink layer which is delicious. Remove all meat and coral, if there is any, from the shell. Break large claws and extract meat from them. Pound or blend all meat with chives, horseradish, cream, lemon juice, butter, salt and pepper. Garnish with sprigs of parsley and wedges of lemon. Serve with home-made brown bread and butter.

Fried Cockles and Rashers

2 litres (3 pints) cockles
225 g (8 oz) rashers
a little pepper

Prepare the cockles by leaving overnight in a bucket of clean, fresh water – this not only cleans them but rids them of excess salt. Drain and rinse in lots of fresh water to make sure all sand is removed. To open, place in a saucepan over a low heat for a few minutes and remove the cockles from their shells.

Meanwhile, fry the rashers until they are crisp. Remove them from the pan and keep warm. Fry the cockles in the rasher fat for about five minutes. Sprinkle with a little pepper and serve immediately with the rashers, all piping hot. *Serves 4.*

Drumlin Country Crayfish Surprise

48 freshwater crayfish
50 g (2 oz) salt
1 onion, peeled and sliced
1 bouquet garni
60 ml (4 tablespoons) Irish
  whiskey

Freshwater crayfish are miniature, olive-green lobsters. They are regarded as a great delicacy. Unfortunately, with increasing pollution in most countries, they have become an expensive and rare delicacy. Luckily they still abound in Ireland's clear waters, particularly in the lakes and streams of the limestone central plain. If you wish, you can easily catch them yourself. All that's necessary is to attach a suitable bait – a none too fresh fish or piece of meat would be ideal – to a stick or a string and drop it into the stream or lake for a few minutes. Remove the bait and you will find the hungry little crayfish clinging to it. Drop them immediately into a bucket of fresh water and continue fishing until you have enough (allow about 12 crayfish per person).

Wash the live crayfish in plenty of water. Pull out the middle tail fin, if possible – this removes the intestine. Boil the onion and bouquet garni for a few minutes. Add the salt. Drop in the crayfish and

·DRUMLIN COUNTRY CRAYFISH SURPRISE·

33

simmer in a lidded saucepan for 5–10 minutes until the crayfish turn red. Drain well and keep warm. Heat the Irish whiskey, set it alight and pour it over the warm, unshelled crayfish. Serve immediately. *Serves 4.*

Crayfish with Dill

4 dozen crayfish
1 onion, peeled and stuck with 2 cloves
a large bunch of dill
600 ml (1 pint) cider
salt
50 g (2 oz) butter
25 g (1 oz) flour

Place onion with cloves, bunch of dill, bay leaf and cider in a saucepan. Add 600 ml (1 pint) of water and salt to taste. Bring to the boil.

Scrub the live crayfish in plenty of fresh water. Remove the middle tail fin, if possible – this removes the intestine. Throw the crayfish into the boiling stock and simmer for 5–10 minutes. Allow to cool. Remove the crayfish and strain the cooking liquid. Bring to the boil again and simmer until it reduces by half. Reserve the bunch of dill and chop.

In a saucepan, melt the butter and stir in the flour. Gradually add 300 ml ($\frac{1}{2}$ pint) of the reduced cooking liquid and cook for 10 minutes, stirring all the time. Add the chopped dill to the sauce. Correct the seasoning. To serve, place the crayfish in a serving dish and pour the sauce over them. *Serves 4.*

Smoked Fish Salad

6 radishes
1 small cucumber
4 stalks celery
2 spring onions
450 g (1 lb) smoked fish
150 ml ($\frac{1}{4}$ pint) mayonnaise
small head of lettuce

Slice well-washed radishes finely. Cut (unpeeled) cucumber and celery into chunks and chop spring onions finely. Remove skin and bones from fish and cut into chunks. Mix fish, vegetables and mayonnaise gently together. Pile into a salad bowl lined with lettuce leaves. *Serves 4.*

Irish Smoked Herrings

4 medium-sized herrings, freshly filletted
150 ml ($\frac{1}{4}$ pint) Irish whiskey

This is one of the two Irish dishes featured in the *Larousse Gastronomique* and so we may conclude that the dish was served very frequently in the nineteenth century. It is one of the simplest and most delicious ways of serving this excellent fish.

Wash and dry the herrings and trim off the heads. Spread them out very flat in a deep dish. Warm the whiskey. **Pour over the herrings and flame. When the whiskey has all burned away and the flames subside, the dish is ready to eat.**

Soused Herrings

4 – 6 herring fillets
1 tablespoon mixed pickling spice
1 cup cider vinegar
1 cup water
a few cucumber chunks
1 teaspoon salt
1 dried bay leaf
1 onion, peeled and sliced

Roll up each fillet with a thin slice of onion and cucumber. Secure with a cocktail stick. Pack into an oven-proof dish. Scatter pickling spice between and over the herrings. Add the remainder of the onion and cucumber. Place the bay leaf in the centre of the dish. Sprinkle with salt and pour in vinegar and water together. Bake in a slow oven (270°F, Gas 1, 140°C) for 1½ hours. *Serves 2–3.*

Oatmeal Herrings

4 fresh herrings
salt and pepper
1 egg, beaten
50 g (2 oz) oatmeal
50 g (2 oz) dripping
parsley sprigs
lemon wedge

Be not sparing,
leave off swearing,
Buy my herring
Fresh from Malahide
Better ne'er was tried.
Come eat 'em with pure fresh butter and mustard,
Their bellies are soft, and white as a custard.
Come, sixpence a dozen to get me some bread,
Or like my own herrings, I shall soon be dead.
(Dean Swift)

Clean, dry and trim the fish. Season the cavities. Score across the fish in two or three places. Brush with beaten egg and then roll in the oatmeal until they are thoroughly coated. Heat the dripping in a heavy-bottomed pan until it is really hot and smoking. Fry the oatmeal-coated herrings carefully until crisp and cooked – this should take about 15 minutes. Serve immediately with parsley sprigs and wedges of lemon. *Serves 4.*

Tartare Sauce

150 ml (¼ pint) mayonnaise
1 dessertspoon chopped gherkins
1 dessertspoon chopped capers
1 dessertspoon chopped parsley

This sauce is invaluable with fried and grilled fish.

Mix all the ingredients together.

450 g (1 lb) angler fish
100 g (4 oz) streaky rashers
225 g (8 oz) mushrooms
a little bacon fat or oil

Angler on a Skewer

The angler in question here is the fish – not the fisherman! (Not all of us would agree with Dr Johnson who, in his dictionary, defined a fishing rod as 'a stick with a worm on one end and a fool on the other.') The firm white flesh of the angler makes it well suited to this preparation – the flesh does not readily flake or fall apart.

Cut the fish and the bacon into bite-size pieces. Clean and trim the mushrooms. Thread on 4 skewers – alternately a piece of fish, a piece of bacon, a mushroom. Brush fish and mushroom with a little bacon fat or oil. Season with pepper. Cook under a hot grill, turning as required – 10 minutes should be sufficient. Serve with wedges of lemon. *Serves 4.*

'CARRAGEEN
FISH MOLD'

12 g (½ oz) carrageen moss
450 ml (¾ pint) fish stock
the rind of 1 lemon, cut into
    matchsticks, and its juice
700 g (1½ lbs) cod or haddock,
    cooked and cut into chunks
1 bunch watercress
4 tomatoes, peeled and quartered
1 onion, peeled and finely sliced

Carrageen Fish Mould

Steep the carrageen moss in cold water for at least 15 minutes. Drain and trim off any discoloured parts. Simmer in fish stock for ½ hour or until the mixture coats the back of a wooden spoon. Add the lemon juice and correct the seasoning.

Pour enough of this mixture into a ring mould (approximately 22.2 cm (8¾) inches in diameter), to coat the base to a depth of about 1 cm (⅜ inch). Set until firm. Cool the remainder. Arrange chunks of fish and matchsticks of lemon rind on the carrageen base. Add the remaining carrageen liquid and leave to set until quite firm. Turn on to a serving dish, and fill the centre of the mould with the watercress, tomatoes and onion rings. Garnish with lemon wedges. *Serves 4–6.*

450 – 700 g (1 – 1½ lb) cod fillet,
    skinned
225 g (8 oz) tomatoes, skinned and
    sliced
½ onion, peeled and sliced
100 g (4 oz) mushrooms, sliced
1 tablespoon parsley, chopped
1 bay leaf or sprig of fennel
sea salt and freshly ground pepper
150 ml (¼ pint) cider

Cider and Cod Stew

Wipe the fish, cut into cubes and lay these in an ovenproof dish. Cover with sliced tomatoes, onions, mushrooms, parsley, bay leaf or fennel, and seasoning. Pour cider over the contents of the dish. Cover with foil and bake in a moderate oven (350°F, Gas 4, 180°C) for 20–25 minutes.

Plaice Casserole

12 small fillets of plaice
salt
a little fresh lemon juice or cider
3 tomatoes
100 g (4 oz) Irish Cheddar Cheese,
    diced
1 onion, peeled and finely chopped
50 g (2 oz) butter

Rub the fillets with salt and lemon juice or cider. Skin the tomatoes – pop for a few seconds into boiling water and the skins will come off easily and quickly – and dice them. Mix diced cheese, onion and tomatoes together. Put a little of the mixture on each fillet, then roll them up. Secure, if necessary, with a cocktail stick. Pack the fillets tightly together in a buttered ovenproof dish. Moisten with a little more lemon juice or cider, and dot with butter. Spread any of the filling mixture left over on top. Bake in a moderate oven (350°F, Gas 4, 180°C) for about ½ hour and serve in dish. *Serves 4–6.*

Fingal's Whiting

2 large onions, peeled and sliced
4 tomatoes, peeled and sliced
700 g (1½ lb) whiting, in 4 pieces
salt and pepper
1 chicken stock cube
2 soupspoonfuls breadcrumbs

Grease an ovenproof dish. Line the bottom of the dish with onion and tomato slices. Lay the whiting pieces over them and season with salt and pepper. Make up chicken stock using stock cube and 300 ml (½ pint) of boiling water. Pour over the fish. Sprinkle with breadcrumbs and dot with butter. Cook in a moderate oven (about 400°F, Gas 6, 200°C) for 30 minutes. During cooking, baste fish a few times. *Serves 4.*

Fish Cakes

225 g (8 oz) fish fillets, poached
450 g (1 lb) cooked potatoes,
    mashed
1 tablespoon parsley, chopped
1 tablespoon chives, chopped
½ teaspoon grated horseradish
2 eggs, beaten
50 g (2 oz) oatmeal
oil and butter for frying

Pound or mince the fish finely. Combine mashed potatoes, herbs, horseradish and fish. Beat all the ingredients together until well mixed. Shape into circular cakes about 3 cm (1 inch) thick and 7.5 cm in diameter. Coat with egg and then oatmeal. Fry in oil and butter until brown and crisp on both sides. Serve piping hot with lots of butter. *Makes about 10 fishcakes.*

Kipper Paste

4 kipper fillets (cooked)
juice and grated rind of 1 lemon
100 g (4 oz) soured cream
15 ml (1 tablespoon) horseradish
    sauce
salt and freshly ground pepper
1 shallot, finely minced

Blend all the ingredients together and serve well chilled.

Inchmore Eel

675 g (1½ lb) eel
50 g (2 oz) butter
1 onion, peeled and chopped
50 g (2 oz) rashers or ham
    chippings

Men since Aristotle have been intrigued by the eel but it was only in 1922 when Dr Schmidt and his research boat, *Dana*, found a young eel off the West Coast of Ireland and a second off the Faeroe Isles that he was on the trail of their birth and death place in the Sargasso Sea, and solved many of the mysteries of this strange and delicious fish.

Inchmore is an island on the Shannon's Lough Ree. The best Lough Ree eels are reckoned to be about 45 to 60 cm (18–20 inches) long.

Clean and skin the eels. Cut into 5 cm (2 inch) pieces. Heat a heavy-bottomed casserole. Put the pieces of eel in the hot casserole and cook gently in their own juices in the lidded casserole for ¼ hour. Lift out the eel. Melt a knob of butter in the casserole and add chopped onion. Cook for a few minutes. Chop the rashers and add to the onion in the pan. Return the eel to the pan and allow to cook for about ½ hour until the eel is really well cooked – the meat should come away from the bones easily. Serve with home-made brown bread. *Serves 4.*

Killaloe Eel Stew

1 kg (2 lbs) eels
50 g (2 oz) butter
1 large onion, peeled and chopped
2 tablespoons flour
600 ml (1 pint) fish stock
salt and freshly ground black
    pepper
1 celery stalk, chopped
1 bay leaf

Skin the eels – make an incision where the skin joins the tail, ease skin away from the flesh and pull firmly towards the head. Chop the eels into small pieces (about 1 inch long) and set aside. Melt the butter in a heavy pan. Add onion and cook until transparent. Stir in the flour slowly and then add the stock. Season and add the celery and bay leaf. Simmer for 15 minutes, put in the eel and simmer for a further 20 minutes. This dish actually improves by being cooked beforehand and left to stand for a while – this helps bring out and blend the different flavours more. *Serves 4.*

Derravaragh Salmon Trout Steaks

4 steaks, about 3 cm (1 inch) thick,
    cut from a medium-sized
    salmon trout, about 1.6 kg (3½
    lb) in weight

Derravaragh, Killarney of the Midlands, harboured the three children of Lir for three hundred years. The children had been changed into swans by their cruel

½ onion, peeled and finely chopped
1 tablespoon parsley, finely
    chopped
100 g (4 oz) mushrooms, finely
    sliced
2 tablespoons fresh dill, chopped
50 g (2 oz) butter

stepmother. There are still plenty of swans on Der-ravaragh, but even more exciting, perhaps, are the magnificent salmon trout, up to ten pounds in weight, and with the most marvellous salmon-pink flesh, which tease the patient angler. The best time for catching them is early summer when the mayflies are hatching on the lake-shore.

Arrange the steaks on four rounds of aluminium foil, large enough to envelop and seal the steak. Place ¼ of the onion, mushroom slices, chopped parsley and dill on each of the steaks. Dot gener-ously with butter. Pull in the edges of the aluminium foil and fold over to make a sealed par-cel. Arrange in an ovenproof dish and bake in a moderate oven (325°F, Gas 3, 160°C) for 20–30 minutes. *Serves 4.*

Glore Trout with Hazelnuts

4 brown trout, about 250 g (10 oz)
    in weight
salt
flour
100 g (4 oz) butter
100 g (4 oz) hazelnuts, halved

The Glore is a wee river whose waters eventually end up in the Shannon. Its unpolluted waters teem with succulent brown trout, and the surrounding wood-land yields a rich harvest of hazelnuts.

After cleaning, make a few incisions in the backs of the fish. Rub in salt and coat with flour. Fry in a little butter until brown on both sides. Put on serv-ing dish and keep warm. Add the rest of the butter and the halved hazelnuts to the pan. Fry very gently for about a minute, then heat carefully until the butter begins to foam. Pour butter and hazelnuts over the trout. Serve immediately. *Serves 4.*

Belfast Salmon Bake

225 g (8 oz) salmon, cooked or
    tinned
100 g (4 oz) breadcrumbs
26 g (1 oz) butter
2 medium eggs, beaten
pepper and salt
1 tablespoon vinegar

This is a favourite old recipe from Northern Ireland, popular when salmon abounded in streams and lakes. Few of us nowadays could afford to prepare fresh salmon in this manner, but the recipe also provides a delicious and different way of serving tinned salmon.

Remove all bones and skin from the salmon and flake the flesh. Rub the breadcrumbs and butter together. Add the beaten eggs, vinegar and flaked

fish. Mix well together and season with lots of pepper and salt. Butter a small shallow pie-dish. Pack the mixture into it and bake in a moderate oven (350°F, Gas 4, 180°C) until nicely browned. Serve with a fresh salad. *Serves 2.*

Poached Salmon

1 kg (2 lb) salmon, middle-cut
1 onion, peeled and sliced
1 stalk celery
1 bay leaf
juice of 1 lemon
salt
3 peppercorns
600 ml (1 pint) water
melted butter
lemon wedges

Add onion, celery, bay leaf, lemon juice, salt and peppercorns to the water. Bring to a boil. Reduce heat and simmer for about 45 minutes to bring out and blend the different flavours. Cool slightly. Carefully place the salmon in stock and bring slowly to simmering point. Remember, a fish boiled is a fish spoiled! 7 minutes' simmering should be adequate. Remove the salmon carefully from the liquid and drain. Serve coated with melted butter and garnished with lemon wedges. *Serves 4–6.*

Collinstown Pike

4 teaspoons butter
1 medium-sized pike, cleaned and patted dry
150 ml (¼ pint) cider
150 ml (¼ pint) cream
2 onions, peeled and finely chopped
salt and pepper
juice of ½ lemon
1 tablespoon chopped parsley

Grease a baking dish with the butter. Cut the cleaned, dry pike in 4 portions and place on the dish. Put cider, cream and chopped onion in a saucepan over moderate heat, and when on the point of boiling, pour over the fish. Bake in a moderate oven (350°F, Gas 4, 180°C) for 30 minutes. The fish should be flaky when cooked. Before serving, correct the seasoning. Add lemon juice and sprinkle with parsley. *Serves 4.*

Parcelled Perch with Herbs

4 perch, (about 225 g (8 oz) each)
salt and pepper
4 sprigs of rosemary
4 sprigs of thyme

Clean and trim the perch. Season the insides with salt and pepper and stuff with sprigs of rosemary, thyme and fennel. Preheat the oven to 450°F, Gas

4 sprigs of fennel
1 onion, peeled and finely chopped
1 tablespoon parsley, finely
  chopped
juice of $\frac{1}{2}$ lemon
100 g (4 oz) butter

8, 230°C. Lay the fish on four pieces of foil, hollow-shaped like boats. Divide over them the finely chopped onion and parsley and dot with butter. Squeeze lemon juice over all. Fold over the edges of the foil carefully to make sealed oval parcels. Cook these parcels in a hot oven for 10 minutes. Cut the sealed top edge off the parcels and serve the fish swimming in its own herb-flavoured juices. *Serves 4.*

·PARCELLED PERCH·

MEATS

Livestock – sheep, goats, lambs and cattle – seems always to have had considerable importance in Ireland. Such was the esteem for roast meats that at all formal banquets, rank and status were indicated by the piece of meat offered. The Hero's Portion was most prized among the up-and-coming young men and many banquets ended in bloodshed and slaughter because of disagreements over this. A king and a poet had the same standing at a banquet – each was entitled to a thigh. A literary sage (would he be a predecessor of a critic?) got a chine. A young lord got a leg, while his lady was presented with a haunch.

One of our earliest and greatest epic sagas, the *Táin Bó Cualaighe*, relates the account of a massive war waged by Ireland's liberated Queen, Maeve of Connaught. The war was caused by the Brown Bull of Ulster, the finest in the land. Maeve thought she might be able to borrow the bull, and offered in exchange to Dara, its owner, fifty heifers, a chariot worth sixty-three cows, and many other marks of her friendship. Unfortunately, things didn't work out so simply and a bloodcurdling war ensued. Maeve, startlingly beautiful and elegant, led her own army.

Later, patriotic poets addressed Mother Ireland with affection and esteem as *a dhruimfhionn donn dilis* ('silk of the kine'). Early in the twentieth century, Francis Ledwidge, lamenting the death of the 1916 rising leader, Thomas MacDonagh, wrote:

But when the Dark Cow leaves the moor
And pastures poor with greedy weeds
Perhaps he'll hear her low at morn
Lifting her horn in pleasant meads.

The Dark Cow referred to is, of course, Ireland.

Borde, a sixteenth century visitor, noticed that 'the Irish cooked their meats in a beast's skin. And the skin shall be set in many stakes of wood, and then they will make a great fire under the skin betwixt the stakes and the skin will not burn greatly. And when the meat is eaten, they for their drink will drink up the broth.' Rowan berries were probably added to the stew.

Irish hospitality knew of no half measures! Egan O'Rahilly praised the hospitality he received in one house; going by his description, nothing seems to have been forgotten.

Meats on spits, and wild fowl from the ocean
Music and song, and drinking bouts;
Delicious roast beef and spotless honey
Hounds and dogs and baying.

Pork, both fresh and salted, seems to have been the commonest meat. Young suckling pigs were spit-roasted for special occasions. The cottiers raised their pigs on acorns and beech mast as well as on scraps and left-overs. Around the feast of St Martin (November 11) the pig was slaughtered. Every smallest scrap of the animal was used and appreciated. Crubeens (or trotters) were and still are regarded as a delicacy. The pig's head made a nice tasty brawn. Meaty spare-ribs, maybe basted with honey and served up with potatoes and cabbage, made a pleasant dinner. The pig's blood, depending on the region, went into either Packet (in Co. Clare) or Drisheens (in Co. Cork). Elsewhere, they were made into tansy-flavoured black puddings (see colour picture on page 82). The stomach was stuffed with good things and baked to become Poor Man's Goose. Then there was the ham and finally the flitches of bacon, salted to a turn, that hung from the smoky rafters in the kitchen and saw the family through the long hard winter. Indeed, beef was often salted and cured too for winter use. Even to-day, corned beef or salt beef and cabbage make a popular dinner. For Christmas, the festive occasion was suitably marked by substituting Spiced Beef for the salty every-day fare.

Strange to say, mutton was seldom eaten, though goat was popular. Even to-day, country folk are very reluctant to eat mutton. Lamb was always regarded as a delicacy. In ancient times, veal was much commoner than it is today. There always was, and still is, the strongest taboo against the eating of horse flesh. An old Irish Penitential is emphatic on the subject: 'Anyone who eats horseflesh does penance for three and a half years.'

Game was plentiful and of a high quality. Today, grouse, snipe, plover, woodcock and pheasant abound. Not only were the red deer, wild boars, hares and rabbits hunted and eaten, but right up to the twentieth century, the badger and the hedgehog were considered a succulent treat.

The Irish had a special way of cooking feathered game or fowl that might be worth trying next time you feel like barbecuing. The bird was coated completely, feathers and all, with a layer of mud paste a couple of inches thick. It was then put into, or under, a hot fire to cook. When it was cooked, it was removed and the mud casing broken. Skin and feathers came away with the mud, revealing a succulent, skinless bird cooked in its own juices. This method was also found useful for cooking hedgehog – it rid one very conveniently of the hedgehog's thorns. From earliest times, it was customary to wrap joints in hay or sedge before cooking. This acted as an insulator, much like aluminium foil today, and prevented the meat from burning. The richly scented meadow with wild garlic, thyme and marjoram would also subtly flavour the joint. (Michel Guérard in his *Cuisine Minceur* is reintroducing the technique to the twentieth century in his recipe for *Gigot d'Agneau Cuit dans le Foin* – Leg of Lamb cooked in Hay.) In the days of the Fianna, simple but effective ovens were built by digging deep pits in the ground. Large stones were heated in the fire. The hot stones were then placed in the pit. The meats were 'buried' among the hot stones. The 'oven' was sealed in with a layer of clay, resulting in the world's most original slow-cooker. Spit-cooking was also popular, using pointed hazel rods for spits and skewers.

CORNED BEEF
AND CABBAGE

COLLEEN'S
HORSERADISH
SAUCE

Irish Spiced Beef

Spiced Beef is part of traditional Christmas fare in Ireland and it is normally bought from the butcher. However, it is quite simple, if a little time-consuming, to prepare oneself.

Ingredients for spicing a 3 kg (7 lb) joint:

3 shallots, chopped
3 bay leaves, pounded
1 teaspoon powdered cloves
1 teaspoon mace
½ teaspoon ground pepper
1 teaspoon allspice
3 teaspoons brown sugar
2 teaspoons saltpetre
450 g (1 lb) sea salt
300 ml (½ pint) Guinness

Combine all the ingredients except the Guinness. Put into a large shallow earthenware container with the meat and rub in the mixture thoroughly. Leave it for at least a week, turning the meat twice. Then tie the meat in muslin to prevent its falling apart during cooking.

To cook, cover the meat with hot water and simmer for 6 hours. During the last hour add the Guinness. When cooked remove from the liquid and press between two dishes with a weight on top. This dish is normally served cold.

Corned Beef and Cabbage

1 kg (2 lb) salt beef brisket
2 bay leaves
freshly ground black pepper
3 large carrots
3 Spanish onions
4 large potatoes, peeled
1 medium head cabbage, quartered
horseradish sauce

Wipe the salt beef and tie in shape. Put into a saucepan with enough cold water to cover. Bring to the boil, drain and rinse beef. If the beef is very salty, it may be necessary to repeat this operation.

Cover the brisket with boiling water; add bay leaves and black pepper. Cover and simmer gently for 1½–2 hours, or until meat is tender. Skim off excess fat. Add carrots, onions and potatoes (sliced), cook for about 20 minutes, then add cabbage wedges. Cook until cabbage and vegetables are tender, but not overdone. Serve the beef surrounded by vegetables, accompanied by horseradish sauce *Serves 4–6.*

Roast Royal Meath Sirloin

1 2–2½ kg (4–5 lb) sirloin, rolled and boned
3–5 tablespoons butter or fat
freshly ground black pepper
salt

Coat the beef generously with butter or fat and sprinkle with freshly ground black pepper. Place the meat on a rack over a roasting pan, fatty side on top – this will automatically baste the joint. Roast in a pre-heated hot oven (425°F, Gas 7, 210°C) for 15–20 minutes to sear the joint quickly on the outside and seal in the juices. Then reduce heat slightly to 325°F, Gas 3, 100°C, and continue to roast, basting frequently. Never pierce the joint

45

with a fork or skewer or juices will escape. Allow 20–25 minutes per pound for medium well-done beef, a little longer if you like it well done.

When the meat is cooked to your liking, remove it from the oven to a warm serving dish. Drain off all fat from the roasting pan. Bring to the boil and reduce pan juices a little. Correct seasoning, serve in a sauce boat with the roast. Serve with roast potatoes and fresh garden peas.

Horseradish Sauce is traditionally served with the Sunday roast of beef. (It's also delicious with grilled salmon or trout.)

Horseradish Sauce

50 g (2 oz) grated horseradish
¼ teaspoon made mustard
1 dessertspoon wine vinegar
300 ml (½ pint) double cream

Mix together all the ingredients, except the cream. Whip the cream until stiff and stir in the horseradish mixture gradually. Refrigerate until required.

Wellington Beef

900 g (2 lb) fillet of beef
salt and freshly ground pepper
25 g (1 oz) butter
a little cooking oil (about ½ tablespoon)
225 g (8 oz) puff pastry
1 egg yolk
1 bunch watercress to garnish

The Iron Duke was born at Trim and married an Irishwoman, Kitty Packenham, Lord Longford's sister from Castlepollard. The illustrious general was what the Irish describe as 'a bad son' – he tended to spurn his Irish origins. Once, on being pressed on the subject of his Irishness, he burst out 'One's being born in a stable doesn't necessarily make one a horse.' He was certainly no gourmet either. His chef, Felix, ran away on him claiming that he couldn't cook for such an undiscerning master even if he were a hundred times a hero. Appropriately, Wellington, coming from the rich beefy plains of Meath, gives his name to a substantial beef dish: Wellington Beef.

•WELLINGTON BEEF•

Rub the fillet with lots of salt and pepper. Heat the butter and the oil in a heavy pan and fry the fillet until well browned all over. Remove carefully from the pan, taking care not to pierce the meat, and leave to cool.

Roll out the pastry thinly and large enough to enclose the fillet. Fold the pastry around the meat. Brush the edges with a little egg yolk and seal the pastry around the meat. Brush the pastry all over with the beaten egg yolk to glaze.

Bake in a hot oven (450°F, Gas 8, 230°C) for 15

minutes. Reduce the heat to moderate (350°F, Gas 4, 180°C) for a further 20–25 minutes.

Serve hot or cold, garnished with watercress. *Serves 4.*

Bricriú's Beef Stew

100 g (4 oz) streaky bacon
1 kg (2 lb) round steak
flour
2 onions, peeled and chopped
2 carrots, scraped and chopped
6 potatoes, peeled
1 stick celery
1 sprig thyme
1 bay leaf
salt and pepper

At Bricriú's feast in Celtic Ireland, they served a fattened cow seven years old; since it was a young calf it had eaten nothing but fresh milk, meadow-hay and corn. It was most succulent!

Cut bacon into $\frac{1}{2}$ inch cubes and fry until the fat runs and they are crisp. Cut the beef into bite-size pieces, dust with flour and brown in bacon fat with chopped onions. Remove the bacon, beef and onions to a heavy-bottomed pan. Add chopped carrots, whole potatoes, celery, thyme and bay leaf. Season to taste. Cover with cold water and simmer gently until meat is tender – about $2\frac{1}{2}$–3 hours. *Serves 6–8.*

Gaelic Steak

1 T-bone or fillet steak
cooking oil or fat
2 tablespoons cream
2 tablespoons Irish whiskey
watercress to garnish

'Beef is the king of meat; beef comprehends in it the quintessence of partridge, of quail, venison, pheasant, plum-pudding and custard.' (Dean Swift)

Prepare the steak and fry in very hot fat or oil. Remove from pan and keep warm. Pour whiskey and cream into the pan, stirring well. Heat thoroughly. To serve, pour over the hot steak and serve garnished with watercress. *Serves 1.*

Cluan Tairbh Stew with Beer

1.25 kg (2$\frac{1}{2}$ lb) lean beef from the rump
2–3 tablespoons rendered bacon or pork fat
450 g (1 lb) sliced onions
300 ml ($\frac{1}{2}$ pint) beef stock
1 tablespoon brown sugar
300 ml ($\frac{1}{2}$ pint) beer
6 parsley sprigs
1 bay leaf

Cut the beef into bite-size pieces and brown quickly in a frying pan in very hot fat. Reduce the heat slightly and add the onions. Brown onions lightly. Put the browned beef and onions in a heavy-bottomed casserole. Heat the stock in frying pan and scrape up the cooking juices. Stir in the brown sugar. Pour over meat. Add enough beer to just cover the meat. Bury the herbs in the stew. Bring to the boil. Reduce heat and simmer gently until meat

1 sprig thyme
1 tablespoon flour
1 tablespoon butter
1 tablespoon parsley, finely
  chopped

is tender – about 2½–3 hours. Remove herb sprigs. Drain cooking liquid off meat. Work about a tablespoon of flour with a tablespoon of butter and drop into cooking liquid to thicken it. Bring to the boil and simmer for 10–15 minutes to cook flour thoroughly. Carefully correct the seasoning. Pour the sauce back over the meat. Garnish with chopped parsley and serve with potatoes. *Serves 4–6.*

Queen Maeve Beef Stew

100 g (4 oz) lean bacon
450 g (1 lb) shin of beef
50 g (2 oz) fat
50 g (2 oz) flour
600 ml (1 pint) brown stock (or use
  stock cube)
1 bay leaf
salt and freshly ground black
  pepper
2 large onions, peeled and sliced
3 large carrots, scraped and sliced
1 small swede turnip, diced
2 sticks celery, sliced

Maeve, Queen of Connaught, was probably the first of Ireland's women's libbers! She ruled her kingdom with an iron hand until the day when she coveted the Ulster King's Brown Bull. The full story of this epic war is told in the *Táin Bó Cualaighe*.

Dice the bacon and cut the beef into 3 cms (1 in) cubes. Heat the fat until it is smoking hot. Throw in meat cubes and fry quickly until brown on all sides and the juices are sealed in. Remove from pan and put in a casserole.

Blend flour in a little of the stock and boil for a few minutes in the pan before pouring, with pan juices, over the meats. Add the rest of the stock, bay leaf, and seasonings. Cook gently in a lidded casserole in a slow oven or on the hot plate for 1½ hours or until the meat is tender. Half an hour before cooking is completed, add sliced onion, carrots, celery and diced swede turnip.

When cooked, skim fat from the surface, correct seasoning and serve with boiled or baked potatoes. *Serves 4–6.*

Irish Stew

1 kg (2 lb) shoulder of mutton
1 kg (2 lb) potatoes
450 g (1 lb) onions
2 stalks celery (optional)
4 white turnips (optional)
salt and freshly ground black
  pepper
water to cover
2–3 tablespoons chopped parsley

Trim off all possible fat from the mutton and cut into 6 cms (2 in) cubes. Peel and thickly slice potatoes and onions. Chop celery and quarter turnips. Place a layer of onions, turnips and celery in the bottom of a heavy casserole; cover with a layer of meat, then a layer of potatoes and continue fitting in alternate layers. Season to taste. Add water to cover. Bring to the boil. Skim. Lower heat and simmer until tender (about 3 hours). Just before serving, sprinkle with chopped parsley. *Serves 4–6.*

Grilled Baby Lamb Chops

8 baby lamb loin chops
1 tablespoon butter
rosemary or oregano
salt and pepper

Preheat grill for 15 minutes. Dot lean part of chop with butter and sprinkle with a little rosemary or oregano and freshly ground pepper. Grill for about 6 minutes on each side, depending on the thickness of the chops. Season with salt and serve immediately. *Serves 4.*

Roast Leg of Lamb and Minty Gravy

4 sprigs fresh mint
1 tablespoon butter
1 leg lamb
3 streaky rashers

Place mint in the bottom of a well-buttered roasting tin. Place leg of lamb on top. Spread rashers over meat. Cook in a moderate oven (350°F, Gas 4, 180°C) allowing 25 minutes to the pound. Baste the joint from time to time. At the end of the cooking time, remove lamb and bacon and keep warm. Skim off all fat from cooking juices in baking tin and remove sprigs of mint. Correct seasoning. Serve in a sauceboat as a thin minty gravy. *Serves 6.*

Creamy Lamb Stew

1.25 kg (2½ lb) shoulder of lamb
600 ml (1 pint) stock
1 teaspoon salt
4 white turnips
1 leek
2 Spanish onions
12 button mushrooms
1 tablespoon butter
1 tablespoon flour
150 ml (¼ pint) cream
juice of ¼ lemon
blade of mace

Cut shoulder of lamb into small pieces and place in a heavy-bottomed casserole with the stock. (If you use stock cubes to make this, remember not to over-salt it.) Bring to the boil. Add turnips, leek and onions. Reduce the heat and simmer gently for 1½ hours or until the meat is tender. Sauté mushrooms in a little butter and lemon juice and keep warm. Remove lamb pieces and vegetables from casserole. Thicken sauce by adding the blended flour and butter. Bring to the boil and simmer for 15 minutes. Finish by stirring in cream and juice of ¼ lemon. Return vegetables, lamb and mushrooms to sauce. Season with a little mace. *Serves 4–6.*

Stuffed Breast of Lamb

1 breast of lamb, boned and
    trimmed
2 tablespoons butter
100 g (4 oz) breadcrumbs
1 small onion, finely chopped
50 g (2 oz) mushrooms, chopped

Mix together breadcrumbs, mushrooms, onion, parsley and dill, marjoram or mace. Season well with salt and pepper. Work butter through and bind with egg. Spread the stuffing over the inside of the breast of lamb. Roll up tightly and tie with string.

1 teaspoon parsley, chopped
a little dill, marjoram or mace
salt and pepper
1 teaspoon butter
1 egg

Place in a small roasting pan and cover with foil. Cook in a hot oven (400°F, Gas 6, 200°C) for the first 30 minutes, then reduce heat to 325°F, Gas 3, 160°C, for 1½ hours. Thirty minutes before the end of cooking time remove foil to crisp the outside. *Serves 4–6.*

Dublin Coddle

Sean O'Casey, Dean Swift and, I'm sure, James Joyce and Brendan Behan all ate and enjoyed the traditional Dublin coddle. The recipe given below is a modern version of the old dish.

225 g (½ lb) onions
3 cooking apples, peeled
225 g (8 oz) rashers
450 g (1 lb) sausage meat
1 leaf sage, finely chopped
pepper
3 cloves
1 cup water or half and half cider
  and water

Skin and slice onions. Peel, core and roughly chop apples. Cut rashers in three. Mix sausage meat, sage and pepper. Mould into sausage-shaped dumplings. Line saucepan with half the onions and apple. Lay out half the rashers and sausages. Sprinkle with apple and onion. Add another layer of rashers and sausage meat and finish off with remainder of apple and onion. Add a few cloves. Pour on water or water and cider. Lay aluminium foil or grease-proof paper on top. Cover with a tight lid and simmer for ¾ hour. *Serves 4.*

· PORK CHOPS
  AND APPLES·

Crubeens

One of the great traditional Irish dishes, crubeens — or pig's trotters — are served with soda bread and stout. They can either be boiled in water with vegetables and aromatics or, split, rolled in beaten egg, then in dry breadcrumbs and fried in bacon fat until crisp and golden. In the latter case, dip in a little mustard and eat with the fingers. Either way, they are delicious.

Boiled Bacon and Cabbage

1 kg (2 lb) streaky bacon
1 white cabbage
black pepper

Soak bacon in cold water for a few hours to remove excess salt. Put it in a saucepan and cover with cold water. Bring slowly to a boil and simmer gently for 1½ hours or until really tender. There is nothing worse than underdone bacon. Turn off the heat and leave bacon to set in the water.

50

Cut the cabbage in quarters. Cut out tough stalks at centre. Wash thoroughly in lots of cold salted water. Rinse then plunge cabbage into fast-boiling water and boil really fast for 3–4 minutes. Add a few cups of the liquid in which the bacon was cooked to salt and flavour cabbage. Continue cooking until cabbage is tender but still crisp. (Traditionally, not much was thought of cabbage cooked without the addition of either meat or meat juices; it was referred to as 'barefooted cabbage' – *cabáiste cosnochtaithe.*)

Slice the bacon and serve with cabbage and a well-flavoured parsley sauce. *Serves 6–8.*

Bacon and Potato Casserole

100 g (4 oz) smoked fat bacon, diced
25 g (1 oz) butter
1 onion, peeled and chopped
25 g (1 oz) flour
700 g (1½ lb) potatoes, peeled and diced
300 ml (½ pint) stock
chopped chives

Fry diced bacon lightly until the fat runs. Add the chopped onion and the diced potatoes and fry over a medium flame until golden brown, adding the butter if necessary. Then stir in the flour and gradually add the stock. Cover, and leave to simmer very gently until cooked and all the liquid is soaked up.

Serve piping hot, garnished with chopped chives. *Serves 4–6.*

Pork Chops and Apples

4 large pork chops, about 1.2 cm (½ inch) thick
300 ml (½ pint) dry cider
1 cup apple sauce
1 teaspoon nutmeg
½ teaspoon salt
2 teaspoons freshly ground pepper

Trim off most of the fat from the pork chops. Combine cider, apple sauce, nutmeg, salt and pepper, stirring well. Marinate the chops in this mixture overnight in the refrigerator. Next day, remove meat from the marinade and drain, but do not dry. Sear under a very hot grill for about 3 minutes on each side. Baste with the marinade and continue cooking, basting and turning at intervals, for about 18 minutes, until the chops are thoroughly cooked. *Serves 4.*

Pork Stew

450 g (1 lb) pork (any cheaper cut)
300 ml (½ pint) water
50 g (2 oz) fat bacon
1 onion, finely chopped

Cut the meat into bite-size pieces and put to simmer in the water for an hour and a half. Allow to cool. Fry the diced fat bacon with finely chopped onion. Work in the flour and cook until the mixture

25 g (1 oz) flour
450 g (1 lb) cooking apples, peeled, cored and sliced
sugar
salt
1–2 tablespoons lemon juice or cider vinegar
1 teaspoon sage, finely chopped

is a rich brown. Little by little, stir in the cooled liquid in which you have cooked the pork. Bring to the boil and then simmer until the sauce thickens.

Flavour the sauce with a little sugar, salt, either lemon juice or cider vinegar and the sage. Pour the sauce over the meat and reheat gently before serving.

Meanwhile make a purée of the apples by cooking them in about 2 tablespoons of cold water. After about 10 minutes, the purée should be ready. Sweeten to taste and serve separately with the stew. *Serves 2–3.*

Pork and Apple Stew

4 shoulder pork chops
3 cooking apples
2 onions
a nut of butter
salt and plenty of pepper
$\frac{1}{4}$ teaspoon allspice
sugar to taste

Trim off all possible fat from chops. Peel, core and slice apples. Skin and slice onions.

Melt butter in a wide ovenproof dish. Put a layer of onion and apple on the bottom and lay chops on this. Sprinkle with pepper and allspice. Put the remaining apple and onion over this. Sprinkle with sugar to taste. Season with salt and pepper. Cover dish and cook in a slow oven for about $2\frac{1}{2}$ hours. Pork needs long slow cooking so this is an ideal dish for cooking in a slow cooker or hay box. *Serves 4.*

Ham in Cider

1 whole ham
2.2 litres (2 quarts) cider
1 bay leaf
$\frac{1}{2}$ cup sugar
cloves
a little brown sugar and breadcrumbs

Steep the ham overnight in cold water.

Line the bottom of a large saucepan with wisps of hay. Put in ham with cider, bay leaf and sugar. If necessary, add enough cold water to cover ham. Bring slowly to a boil. Reduce heat and simmer gently, allowing 20–25 minutes per pound cooking time. Above all don't let the ham cook quickly or it will be tough and ruined. At the end of cooking, let ham set for about 1 hour in the liquid. Carefully take out of pot and remove skin. Coat fat on ham with breadcrumbs mixed with brown sugar and stud with cloves. Brown in a hot oven.

Casseroled Heart

1 ox heart
50 g (2 oz) fat or oil

Slice heart, remove tubes and wash thoroughly. Fry in hot fat until brown, then put in casserole.

2 onions, peeled and sliced
25 g (1 oz) flour
30 ml (½ pint) stock
2 sprigs of thyme
225 g (8 oz) carrots, peeled and grated
½ small swede, peeled and grated
1 tablespoon tomato purée

450 g (1 lb) lamb's liver
25 g (1 oz) flour
salt and pepper
50 g (2 oz) butter
2 onions, peeled and sliced
50 g (2 oz) mushrooms, peeled and sliced
1 small carrot, peeled and diced
1 clove garlic, peeled and crushed
1 beef stock cube
300 ml (½ pint) water

450 g (1 lb) streaky bacon rashers
2 large onions, sliced
2 small white heads of cabbage
4 partridges
4 small onions stuck with cloves
1 carrot, sliced
salt and pepper
stock
bouquet garni
6 juniper berries
½ glass cider

Brown onions and add to casserole. Add flour to fat and brown. Pour in the stock. Boil for a few minutes, add thyme. Then pour over meat in casserole. Cover and cook in oven at 300°F, Gas 2, 150°C for 2½–3 hours. Add carrots and swede and cook for a further hour. *Serves 4.*

Braised Liver

Trim the liver and toss in seasoned flour. Brown well on both sides in the butter in a heavy-bottomed pan. Remove to a casserole. Sauté sliced onions and mushrooms. Place over liver with diced carrot. Crush garlic clove in a little salt and add to liver. Crush stock cube in water and pour over liver and vegetables. Add the tomato purée. Cook in a moderately hot oven (375°F, Gas 5, 190°C) for 45 minutes. *Serves 4.*

Partridge with Cabbage

Partridge should be hung for at least 4 days to develop its delicate flavour. Since the birds are small – between 300 – 350 g (12 – 14 oz) each – allow one bird per serving. A young partridge is usually roasted as described in the recipe for roast grouse   but for more senior birds this recipe works well.

Dice all except four of the rashers. Put into a heavy casserole with half the sliced onions. Blanch the cabbage by parboiling it for a few minutes and then plunging into cold water. Cut each head into eight pieces and remove tough stalks. Lay half the cabbage on the ingredients in the casserole. Wrap each bird in a rasher. Place a small onion stuck with a clove on the cabbage in the casserole. Cover with the remaining cabbage and sliced onions, and the carrot. Season with salt and pepper and add enough stock to cover. Put in bouquet garni and juniper berries. Bring to the boil and then simmer until really tender. About ¼ hour before the end of cooking, add the cider.
**   To serve, arrange vegetable mixture on a hot platter with the partridges on top. Strain the gravy and boil for a few minutes to reduce slightly. Correct seasoning and pour over the birds.** *Serves 4.*

Poor Man's Goose

900 g – 1.4 kg (2 – 3 lb) liver, in one
   piece
225 g (8 oz) breadcrumbs
1 onion, finely chopped
225 g (8 oz) lean bacon, minced
parsley
a little sage
salt and pepper
a little milk
225 g (8 oz) fat bacon rashers

This dish is also known as 'mock goose'. Traditionally, after the slaughter of the pig, one of the helpers was given the pig's stomach and it was in this stomach bag that the poor man's goose was cooked.

Slit the liver half through and then crossways without cutting right through. Mix the crumbs with the chopped onion and minced bacon. Add parsley, a hint of sage and salt and pepper to taste. Moisten the stuffing with a little milk. Pack into the slits in the liver and sew up to make a 'goose'. Place on a tray in the roasting pan. Pour a cup of boiling water into the pan. Cover the liver with rashers. Put aluminium foil over all and cook in a moderate oven (350°F, Gas 4, 180°C) until tender. This should take about $1\frac{1}{4}$ hours. Just before taking from the oven, remove the rashers and allow the top of your 'goose' to brown slightly. Remove the 'goose' from the oven. Pour off fat from the pan juices, strain some of this gravy over the goose and serve the rest in a sauceboat. *Serves 6–8.*

Grouse Casserole

2 – 4 grouse
300 ml ($\frac{1}{2}$ pint) dry cider
25 g (1 oz) flour
salt and freshly ground black
   pepper
olive oil
1 clove garlic, crushed
225 g (8 oz) mushrooms, sliced
1 onion, sliced
pinch of cayenne pepper
sprig of thyme

Marinate the grouse in cider for at least 24 hours. When ready to cook, remove from the marinade, dry and coat in seasoned flour. Brown in a little oil and remove to a heavy casserole. Cover with the marinade. Add crushed garlic, sliced mushrooms, onion, cayenne pepper and thyme. Bring to the boil. Cover and simmer until the meat is tender and lifts off the bone easily. This, depending on age of the grouse, may take between 30 and 45 minutes. Red cabbage cooked with apples makes an excellent accompaniment to this casserole. *Serves 2–4.*

Roast Grouse

2 grouse
50 g (2 oz) butter
2 streaky rashers
2 slices fried bread or toast

Roasting is a method really suitable only for young birds, easily recognized by their soft pliable feet and the end of the breast bone, which in all young birds is also pliable. By nature, grouse are extremely dry birds, so it is a good idea to wrap the birds in a streaky rasher and place a knob of butter in the cavity. A

2 plump pigeons, quartered
50 g (2 oz) butter
50 g (2 oz) fat bacon
flour
grated rind and juice of one lemon
1 shallot, finely chopped
150 ml ($\frac{1}{4}$ pint) beef stock
salt and freshly ground black
    pepper

50 g (2 oz) lard
50 g (2 oz) fat bacon, diced
1 large onion, finely chopped
4 pigeons
1 Bramley seedling or cooking
    apple, peeled and chopped
6 juniper berries
salt and freshly ground black
    pepper
125 ml ($\frac{1}{4}$ pint) red wine
600 ml (1 pint) good stock

small onion stuck with a few cloves may also be placed inside to add flavour.

Place the bacon-covered grouse on a rack in the roasting pan and roast in a hot oven (400°F, Gas 6, 200°C) for 15 minutes. Reduce the heat to moderate (350°F, Gas 4, 180°C) and continue cooking until the birds are tender, about another 15–20 minutes. Baste frequently. Five to ten minutes before the end of cooking, remove the bacon to allow skin to crisp. Remove birds from the oven. Collect dripping from the pan and spread over the slices of fried bread. Serve the birds on the fried bread, garnished with watercress. *Serves 2.*

Pigeon and Bacon Pie

Remove the pigeons' innards, but retain the livers and chop them. Heat butter in a saucepan and brown the quartered pigeons in it. Dice the bacon and add with the chopped livers. Dredge with flour and brown all over. Add lemon rind and juice, shallot, stock, salt and pepper. Cover and simmer gently until pigeons are really tender – this will depend on the age of the birds. Serve the pigeons in their sauce with crisp slices of fried bread. *Serves 4.*

Casseroled Pigeons

Pigeons abound in Ireland. They are meaty little birds and make really good eating. The flesh tends to be dry so if you want to grill or roast them it is best to lard them or marinate them beforehand.

Melt the lard in a fire-proof casserole over moderate heat. Add bacon and onion and cook until the onion begins to brown. Cut the pigeons cleanly in half down the backbone. Add pigeon halves and brown on both sides. As they brown, remove from pan and keep warm. Add apple, juniper berries, salt and pepper. Lay pigeons and fried onions on top. Pour wine and stock over all, cover and cook in a moderate oven (300°F–350°F, Gas 2 or 3, 150°C-160°C) for about 2 hours, or until pigeons are tender, depending on the age of the birds. *Serves 8.*

Yogurt Pigeon Stew

4 pigeons
450 ml (¾ pint) cider
juice of ½ lemon
225 g (½ lb) bacon, diced
salt and freshly ground black
    pepper
½ cup of yogurt

Cut pigeons in four. Mix cider and lemon juice together and pour over the pigeons. Add the diced bacon and season with salt and pepper. Cover and cook in a moderate oven (350°C, Gas 4, 180°C) for about 45 minutes. Then spoon yogurt over the pigeons. Cover and continue cooking for another 15 minutes. Serve with creamed potatoes. *Serves 6–8.*

Braised Pheasant with Apples

1 pheasant
675 g (1½ lb) cooking apples
100 g (4 oz) butter
150 g (¼ pint) cream

Split the pheasant in two through the back, separating the halves. Peel, core and thickly slice the apples. Heat the butter in a pan and brown the pheasant all over. Remove it and put in the apples and brown slightly. Put a layer of apples in the bottom of a casserole. Place the pheasant and the rest of the apples on top. Pour the cream all over. Cover and cook in a moderate oven (350°F, Gas 4, 180°C) for about 1 hour, or until the pheasant is quite tender. *Serves 2–3.*

Roast Pheasant with Yogurt Sauce

2 young pheasants
50 g (2 oz) breadcrumbs
sherry
100 g (4 oz) hazelnuts, crushed
12 juniper berries
1 teaspoon grated orange peel
melted butter
salt and pepper
½ onion, finely chopped
150 ml (¼ pint) cider
150 ml (¼ pint) yogurt
dill

Moisten the breadcrumbs with the sherry. Add crushed hazelnuts, 6 juniper berries, orange peel, salt and pepper. Stuff birds with this mixture. Place birds on rack in a roasting pan. Brush with lots of butter and sprinkle with salt and pepper. Put into a very hot oven (425°F, Gas 7, 220°C) for 10 minutes. Lower the heat to hot (400°C, Gas 6, 200°C) and continue cooking until tender. Remove birds and keep warm. Add finely chopped onion and remaining juniper berries to pan and fry until nice and brown. Stir in the cider and then gradually add the yogurt. Continue cooking. Add dill to taste. Correct seasoning. When sauce is really hot, pour some over the pheasants. Serve the remainder separately in a sauceboat. *Serves 4–6.*

Roast Snipe

3 or 4 snipe
100 g (4 oz) bacon rashers
butter
3 shallots, chopped
sprig of parsley, chopped
150 ml ($\frac{1}{4}$ pint) red wine
several rounds of fried bread
a little sour cream

Remove the insides from the birds, reserving the liver and heart. Do not cut the heads off. Tuck their long beaks underneath and wrap each bird in a rasher of bacon. Put them, with a little butter, in a roasting tin and roast in a hot oven (425°F, Gas 7, 220°C) for about 20 minutes. Chop the livers and hearts. Mix with shallots and parsley and cook in the pan juices until well cooked. Add the wine and a little sour cream. Fry for a minute or so. Serve the birds surrounded by slices of fried bread garnished with the liver mixture. *Serves 2–3.*

Roast Michaelmas Goose

1 4 kg (9 lb) oven-ready goose
1 medium onion
1 cup stock
salt and pepper

For the Stuffing
450 g (1 lb) cooking apples, peeled and chopped
50 g (2 oz) butter
$\frac{1}{2}$ onion, chopped
100 g (4 oz) celery, chopped
250 g ($\frac{1}{2}$ lb) breadcrumbs
salt and pepper

'If you eat goose on Michaelmas Day, you will never want money all the year round.' (Proverb)

Select a plump goose with clear yellow beak and feet. Remove the excess fat from the cavity. Trim off the neck close to the body. Cut off wings and feet at the first joint. Rub the goose all over with a little salt. An apple stuffing goes very well with goose.

Mix all the stuffing ingredients together thoroughly. If liked, the goose liver may be chopped up and added to it. Stuff the goose.
     Put the goose on a rack in a large roasting pan. Put a little boiling water and an onion in the pan. Cover the bird with greased paper and roast in a moderate oven (350°F, Gas 4, 180°C) allowing about 25 minutes per pound cooking time. Baste frequently. During the last $\frac{1}{2}$ hour, pour $1\frac{1}{2}$ tables-

poons cold water all over the breast to make the skin brown and crusty. When goose is tender, take it from the pan and place on a hot dish.

To make the gravy: pour off most of the fat, add the hot stock and scrape around the bottom and edges of the pan. Season with salt and pepper, bring to the boil, strain and serve.

Rabbit Stewed in Cider

1 rabbit
juice of ½ lemon
100 g (4 oz) streaky bacon, diced
seasoned flour
3 large onions, peeled and chopped
sprig of thyme
1 bay leaf
a few sprigs of parsley
450 g (1 lb) tomatoes, skinned and chopped
sea-salt and freshly ground pepper
15 g (½ oz) sugar
300 ml (½ pint) dry cider

Cut rabbit into serving pieces and soak for a few hours in cold water to which the lemon juice has been added. Drain and dry. Fry bacon gently until the fat runs. Remove the bacon and keep warm. Toss rabbit portions in seasoned flour and fry until golden brown. Add onions, thyme, bay leaf, parsley and tomatoes. Fry gently for 15–20 minutes. Add salt, pepper and sugar, then add cider. Bring to the boil for 3–5 minutes, then reduce the heat and cook in a covered pan until the rabbit is tender. Remove thyme, bay-leaf and parsley before serving. *Serves 4.*

Hare Stew

1 hare
225 g (½ lb) onions
225 g (½ lb) bacon, diced
25 g (1 oz) flour
1 bay leaf
pinch of nutmeg and cinnamon
150 ml (¼ pint) port wine or red wine
stock or water
100 g (¼ lb) mushrooms, quartered
1 tablespoon redcurrant jelly

Joint the hare. Peel and chop the onion. Sauté the diced bacon in pan until the fat runs. Add onions and continue to sauté until brown. Remove onion and bacon and brown the pieces of hare in the same fat. Sprinkle with flour and continue to brown. Add bay leaf, cinnamon, nutmeg and port or wine with bacon and onions and enough stock or water to cover. Season with freshly ground black pepper. Cover casserole and simmer for 2½–3 hours, depending on the age of the hare. 20 minutes before the end of the cooking time, add the quartered mushrooms and redcurrant jelly. *Serves 4–6.*

Venison Rolls

2 streaky rashers
100 g (4 oz) minced beef
1 small onion, finely chopped
100 g (4 oz) mushrooms, chopped
50 g (2 oz) butter

Remove rinds from rashers and cut in half lengthwise. Fry minced beef, chopped onion and mushrooms in butter for a few minutes. Stir in the breadcrumbs and season. Spread a little of the

58

50 g (2 oz) breadcrumbs
salt and pepper
4 thin venison steaks
25 g (1 oz) flour
300 ml (½ pint) beef stock
1 tablespoon rowan jelly

stuffing on each steak. Roll up and wrap in half-rasher. Brown rolls in a heavy-bottomed pan over high heat, adding a little extra butter if necessary. Dust with flour. Add stock, salt and pepper. Simmer for about an hour, or until tender. Remove rolls from pan and stir in rowan jelly (see below) Serve hot with baked potatoes. *Serves 4.*

Venison Cooked in Guinness

1 kg (2 lb) piece of venison
600 ml (1 pint) Guinness
50 g (2 oz) brown sugar
50 g (2 oz) honey
sea salt and freshly ground pepper

Trim off fat and fibre – deer fat is unpleasant and gives a goat-like taste if not removed. Marinate the venison in Guinness for 24 hours at least – longer if you like a gamier taste. Put venison, Guinness, sugar and honey in a heavy-bottomed casserole. Season. Bring to a boil for two to three minutes. Reudce the heat and cook gently for about an hour, or until meat is tender. This will depend on the age of the animal, the length of time hanging, etc. *Serves 4–6.*

Donegal Rowan Jelly

450 g (1 lb) rowan berries
450 g (1 lb) crab apples
sugar

A medieval Ossianic tale tells us of the rowan tree: 'Every berry that comes on that tree has great virtues. There is the intoxication of wine and the satisfaction of old mead in each berry and whoever eats three of those berries, even if he were a hundred years old, his age would return to ten and twenty years.' The flamboyantly coloured fruit of the mountain ash or rowan tree has for centuries brightened the rugged Donegal mountains. This Donegal rowan jelly is delicious served with roast mutton or venison. Fionn and the Fianna probably served their game with a relish of rowan berry.

Barely cover the fruit with water and simmer until tender. Strain into a jelly-bag or through several thicknesses of muslin. Measure the liquid and allow 450 g (1 lb) of sugar to every 600 ml (1 pint) of juice. Heat the required amount of sugar, add to the juice, bring to a rolling boil and continue boiling until setting point is reached. Pot and cover immediately.

59

Burren Roast Kid

1 kid, ideally about 4 or 5 weeks
old, skinned
125 g (¼ lb) butter
marjoram and a sprig of rosemary

For the marinade
1.2 litres (2 pints) buttermilk

The Burren in Co. Clare is an extraordinary place, its karstic landscape distorted and tortured by wild Atlantic winds. Herds of wild goats still roam there, eking out an existence on the sparse but exotic plants that flourish in nooks and crannies: gentians, wild irises and orchids as well as the many grasses and lichens that make this a botanist's paradise. Traditionally, many of the kids are killed for Easter Sunday's lunch.

Since the meat of kid is extremely dry, marinate it for about one day in buttermilk, turning frequently to ensure the marinade thoroughly penetrates the meat.
   When ready to cook, remove from the buttermilk, dry well and coat generously all over with butter. Sprinkle the marjoram both inside and outside the carcase. Wrap in a large sheet of aluminium foil and roast in a moderate oven (350° F gas 4, 275°C) for 1½–2 hours according to size *Serves 6–8.*

Viking Wild Duck

1 wild duck
2 tablespoons oil
150 ml (¼ pint) soured cream or
yogurt
150 ml (¼ pint) milk

For the sauce
50 g (2 oz) butter
15 ml (1 tablespoon) flour
salt and pepper
1 tablespoon blackcurrant jelly

Rub the bird all over with salt and pepper. Brown all over in a heavy casserole. Pour the sour cream and the milk all over it. Cover with a lid and simmer for 45 minutes or 1 hour. Remove the duck and keep warm. To make the sauce, melt the butter and stir in the flour, cook until it is light brown. Slowly add some of the strained liquid from the casserole. Stir, then cook for 10 minutes. Season with salt and pepper and stir in the blackcurrant jelly. Serve the sauce separately. *Serves 4.*

Roast Duckling

1 1.8 kg (4 lb) duckling
225 g (½ lb) cooking apples
2 tablespoons honey
salt and pepper

Remove as much fat as possible from the duckling. Wash and dry the bird thoroughly. Rub with salt and pepper. Place on a rack, breast side up, in a fairly hot oven (400°F, Gas 6, 200°C). Pour a little boiling water in the roasting pan after 10–15 minutes, to prevent the melting fat and juices from burning. Reduce the heat after 20 minutes to 350°F,

Gas 4, 180°C and roast for about an hour, basting every 10 minutes.

Meanwhile, peel and core the apples, slice into thick rounds and poach in a little water with the honey, until tender but not mushy. Remove duck from oven and place on a hot serving dish. Skim off fat from roasting pan. Add some of the juice from apples. Thicken the sauce with a little flour. Correct seasoning. Serve the duck garnished with apple rounds and serve the sauce separately. *Serves 3–4.*

Farmhouse Chicken Stew

1 chicken, weighing about 1.5 kg (3½ lb)
salt and pepper
oil or butter
100 g (4 oz) bacon
3 onions, peeled and halved
2 carrots, peeled and sliced
2 celery stalks, chopped
2 potatoes, peeled and chopped
1 sprig thyme
1 bay leaf
parsley
600 ml (1 pint) chicken stock

Skin and joint the chicken and season with salt and pepper. Fry the bacon pieces in a heavy pan until crips and golden. Remove bacon to casserole. Fry onions and carrots in their fat adding a little oil or butter if necessary – for a few minutes before adding to the casserole with the chopped celery, potatoes, thyme, bay leaf and parsley. Pour the stock over the chicken pieces. Cover the casserole and simmer over a low heat until very tender, about 45 minutes–1 hour. *Serves 4–6.*

Chicken and Mushroom Pie

'Promises and pie-crusts are made to be broken.' (Dean Swift)

1 roasting chicken, weighing about 1.5 kg (3½ lb)
salt and freshly ground pepper
1 onion, peeled and finely chopped
100 g (4 oz) cooked ham, chopped
100 g (4 oz) mushrooms, sliced
1 stick celery, finely chopped
1 teaspoon parsley, finely chopped
1 chicken stock cube
300 ml (½ pint) boiling water
225 g (8 oz) short crust pastry
a little milk for glazing

Skin and cut the chicken into joints. Lay them in a pie-dish. Season with salt and pepper. Add onion, ham, mushrooms, celery and parsley. Dissolve stock cube in water. Blend flour in a little water. Add to the stock and bring to the boil. Pour over the chicken. Roll out the pastry and cover the pie. Brush with a little milk and bake in a hot oven (425°F, Gas 7, 220°C) for 30 minutes. Reduce heat to 350°F, Gas 4, 180°C and cook for a further 15–20 minutes. *Serves 4–6.*

Chicken Potato Salad

225 g (8 oz) potatoes, boiled in their skins
1 small cauliflower

Peel and dice the potatoes, trim the cauliflower and break into small florets, cutting off stalks. Soak in cold water with a little of the lemon juice. Wash but

61

2 tablespoons lemon juice
1 red dessert apple
1 small green pepper
1 kg (2 lb) cooked chicken
150 ml ($\frac{1}{4}$ pint) mayonnaise
75 ml (4 tablespoons) cream
salt
$\frac{1}{4}$ teaspoon curry powder

do not peel the apple, remove core and cut into $\frac{1}{2}$ inch dice. Put into a small bowl and sprinkle with lemon juice. Wash the green pepper, cut in half and remove seeds. Cut in $\frac{1}{4}$ inch wide strips. Soak for 2 minutes in boiling water. Remove meat from chicken carcass and cut into bite-size pieces.

Mix mayonnaise, cream, $\frac{1}{4}$ level teaspoon salt and curry powder together. Mix chicken, cauliflower, apple and lemon juice, green pepper and diced potatoes. Mix into creamy sauce until all the ingredients are lightly coated. *Serves 6–8.*

Chicken Irish Mist

1.75 kg (4 lb) farm chicken,
    divided into 8 pieces
a little flour, salt and pepper
75 g (3 oz) butter
150 ml ($\frac{1}{4}$ pint) white stock

For the sauce
3–4 tablespoons Irish Mist
1 small carton double cream
25 g (1 oz) flaked almonds, roasted
    until golden brown
3 dessert apples

Divide the chicken into 8 pieces: two legs, two wings, two pieces from the back and two breasts. Roll them in seasoned flour and fry in very hot butter on both sides. When well coloured, add the stock, cover and simmer for 35 minutes. Remove the chicken pieces to a serving dish.

Make the sauce by adding the Irish Mist to the stock in the pan. Stir in the cream and add the roasted, flaked almonds. Peel the apples, cut them into cubes and cook in the sauce until barely soft. To serve, cover the chicken with the sauce and garnish with the apples. *Serves 4.*

Journey's End Breast of Chicken

4 chicken breasts
100 g (4 oz) flour, seasoned with
    salt
50 g (2 oz) butter
75 ml ($\frac{1}{8}$ pint) cream
2 tablespoons chives, chopped
75 ml ($\frac{1}{8}$ pint) Irish whiskey.

In the remotest and most romantic spot imaginable, Ina Managhan runs a marvellous restaurant. She bakes all her own bread, serves her customers with lots of glistening, freshly caught fish from the Atlantic. I think this recipe she gave me for breast of chicken is as impressive and delicious as it is easy to prepare.

Skin the chicken breasts and toss in the seasoned flour. Melt the butter in a heavy pan and fry the chicken gently in the butter until golden brown. Only a few minutes cooking is required to cook the chicken. Pour in the cream and simmer gently until it is heated through, taking care not to let it boil. Stir the chives into the sauce. Warm the whiskey. Pour over the chicken and sauce. Flame and serve while still flaming.

Chicken with Cream

1 chicken, weighing about 1.5 kg
    (3½ lb)
150 ml (¼ pint) cider
1 bay leaf
1 onion, stuck with a few cloves
salt
25 g (1 oz) flour
25 g (1 oz) butter
6 tablespoons cream
1 large dessert apple, diced

Place chicken in a large saucepan and pour over the cider. Add water to cover, add bay leaf, onion and a little salt. Cover tightly and simmer for about 1 hour or until the chicken is tender. Skin and cut into serving pieces. Blend flour and butter. Moisten with cooking liquid from the saucepan, about 450 ml (¾ pint). Bring to a boil and cook for several minutes to thicken slightly. Add cream and simmer for another minute. Add diced apple to the sauce. Heat thoroughly – the apple should retain a little crunchiness to add texture as well as flavour. Pour over the chicken pieces and serve really hot. *Serves 4–6.*

Chicken with Honey and Pineapple

1 chicken, weighing about 1.5 kg
    (3½ lb)
100 g (4 oz) butter
50 g (2 oz) hazelnuts
350 g (12 oz) tin of pineapple rings
6 tablespoons honey

Cut the chicken into five pieces. Melt the butter and mix with the honey. Pierce the chicken here and there with a sharp-pointed knife and coat with the butter-honey mixture. Heat grill. Grill chicken pieces until cooked through and golden, basting occasionally with pan juices. Chop hazelnuts and toast gently under the grill for a minute or two. Remove chicken pieces and arrange on a heated serving dish. Sprinkle with hazelnuts and garnish with heated pineapple rings. Just before serving, pour the hot juices from the grill pan over the chicken pieces. *Serves 5.*

Miller's Meat Roll

900 g (2 lb) beef, minced
900 g (2 lb) ham, minced
900 g (2 lb) breadcrumbs
1 level teaspoon mixed spice
a little grated nutmeg
2 large (or 3 small) eggs, slightly
    beaten
100 g (4 oz) flour (approx.)
100 g (4 oz) toasted breadcrumbs

For four generations at least, Mrs Joe Miller of Mountrath assures me, the Miller family have prepared vast quantities of this meat loaf for Christmas. On Christmas Eve, all the neighbours and friends congregate in the Miller home to drink the traditional Christmas toast and enjoy a few thick slices of Meat Roll.

Mix the beef, ham, breadcrumbs, spices and nutmeg together. Bind with the slightly beaten eggs. Break the mixture into three 900 g (2 lb) rolls. Liberally cover three boiled pudding cloths with the flour. Stitch the meat rolls into these pudding cloths.

Drop the rolls into a large pan of boiling water and simmer gently for 4 hours. Then lift out the rolls from the pan, remove from the pudding cloths. Roll in the toasted bread crumbs. Allow to stand for at least a few hours in the bottom of the refrigerator before serving chilled.

White Puddings

450 g (1 lb) oatmeal
100 g (4 oz) lard, minced
1 onion, peeled and finely chopped
$\frac{1}{2}$ teaspoon pepper
$\frac{1}{2}$ teaspoon allspice
2–3 sprigs tansy (sage may be substituted)
$\frac{1}{2}$ teaspoon salt
sausage skins

Sausages and puddings were always a favourite dish in Ireland. They were known as *maróc* or *indrectan*, and were boiled after making, so as to half-cook them, and were then put aside until needed. Before serving, they were fried and served piping hot. Tansy, which grows wild in abundance in Ireland, was a favourite flavouring for pork dishes and sausages.

Spread the oatmeal in a dry pan and roast in a hot oven until brown and crisp. Remove from the oven. Stir in the minced lard, onion and seasonings. Pack into well-greased skins – your local friendly pork butcher will be delighted to supply skins – and tie with string. Prick the skin here and there with a fork and set to cook very gently for 1–1$\frac{1}{2}$ hours in lots of salted water. If the skins aren't readily available, pack the mixture into a double thickness of muslin and cook as if in skins. When cooked, hang up to dry.

To fry, cut a slice about 0.6 cms ($\frac{1}{4}$ inch) thick, coat with flour, and fry in a hot pan in bacon fat until crisp and brown.

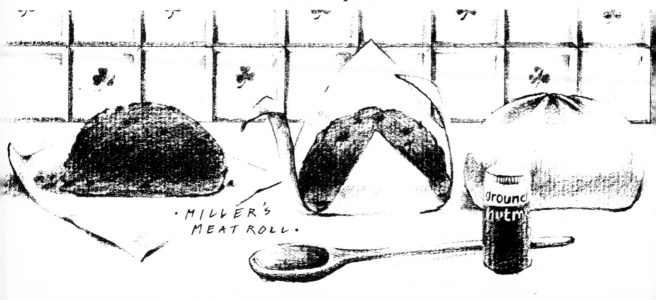

· MILLER'S MEAT ROLL ·

ground nutmeg

VEGETABLES

We have the very best vegetables in the world and the worst cooks. If the young woman will see that her man is fed on a largely vegetable diet she will have a better-tempered husband, for vegetable-eating animals do not bite so much as the carnivorous animals do. (Sir Bruce Porter)

If Sir Bruce's theory were true, the Irish should have long been a very malleable race, since for centuries they lived mainly on vegetables. Meat was something that usually only appeared on the tables of the big houses, except for the Michaelmas Goose, Spiced Beef for Christmas (turkey for Christmas is comparatively modern) and maybe the occasional hare or pigeon during the summer. When the pig was killed at the Big House, the cottiers – if they were lucky – might get a portion of a flitch and that would suffice to garnish and flavour their potatoes and cabbage.

An Irishman is probably the world's best judge of a potato: Kerr's Pinks, Champions, Aran Banners, Golden Wonders, Dates – each of the various varieties have their merits and demerits. Boxty, rasp, colcannon, champ . . . all dishes much appreciated where the potato is king. But if you really want to taste the most delicious potatoes in the world, you must head for Inishmaan (the least accessible of the Aran Islands). There, in Mrs Mulkerrins' guesthouse, you will taste potatoes as they should be. It isn't due just to the *bean a' ti*'s (the hostess's) excellent cuisine: it is due to centuries of cultivation, patient and painstaking, on a bed of sea-weed, sheltered, salvaged almost, from the raging Atlantic with ubiquitous stone walls. The salt and iodine-rich seaweed produces a potato that surpasses all others. Small wonder that Irishmen hastened to introduce the potato to their Scottish neighbours.

Salsify and Jerusalem Artichokes, once very popular in Ireland, are only now coming in for a slow revival. Horseradish, too, seems to have been held in far greater esteem in bygone times. Cabbage, as everyone knows, is one of the mainstays of Irish cuisine, but a glance at Irish literature from the Fionn MacCuil sagas to Oliver Goldsmith would suggest that until then, sorrel and watercress were the chief leaf vegetables.

> She, wretched matron, forced in age, for bread
> To strip the brook with mantling cresses spread.
> (Oliver Goldsmith)

Perhaps its fall from favour had to do with the pollution of streams and an increased awareness of the dangers of fluke in wild watercress.

Did you know that Ireland's woods in late summer and early autumn teem with the most delicious mushrooms: big golden ceps, all soft and spongy and lemon yellow underneath? Try them sliced and fried with potatoes, grilled with fish or baked in cream. Chanterelles are egg-yolk yellow and unmistakable with their funnel shape and delightful fruity smell. They abound in the many lush woodlands throughout the country. Their eggy colour suggests an egg preparation: try them in scrambled egg, or serve them with steak. Lawyer's Wigs (also known as Inky Caps because of their habit of dissolving into a black ink) are simply everywhere in late summer. Pick them really young and use immediately before they start to dissolve and make a terrific mess! Unfortunately, their flavour isn't as delicious as that of other mushrooms. They are ideal for making ketchup. Blewits, puff-balls, Jew's Ears and even – so the connoisseurs assure me, though I've never managed to find them myself – the aristocrats of the mushroom world, morels and truffles, are just waiting to be gathered to add texture, flavour and excitement to your most ordinary dishes. All you need is to arm yourself with a reliable guide (of the 200 or so mushrooms available, about four varieties might be fatal, so don't take chances) and head to the nearest wood to discover, like Louis XVI, 'delights you never dreamt existed'.

Knockferry Red Cabbage

2 onions, peeled and minced
fat for frying
1 large red cabbage, shredded
25 g (1 oz) icing sugar
3 apples, shredded
1 tablespoon caraway seed
300 ml (½ pint) vinegar
salt and pepper to taste

· K N O C K F E R R Y
R E D   C A B B A G E ·

Desmond Moran serves traditional Irish Spiced Beef and red cabbage all the year round at his Farm Guesthouse in Co. Galway and finds his guests appreciate it just as much hot as cold. Here is his recipe for spicy red cabbage.

Fry the onions in a large saucepan with the lid on until they are transparent. Add the cabbage and cook for a while with the lid on, stirring occasionally, then add the other ingredients, the vinegar last. Stir again. Add enough water to keep the cabbage from burning and cook with the lid on until tender, stirring often. *Serves 4–6.*

Portaferry Stewed Dulse

Dulse or *duilisc* (the name comes from a Gaelic word *duill* meaning a leaf and *uisce* meaning water) was always considered of great economic importance, and has for long been harvested along the west coast of Ireland, particularly in the harbour of Cape Clear. Its taste, not unlike roasted oysters, was regarded as a great delicacy by the Fianna of Ireland. Purple Laver, a red seaweed, high in protein, also known as sloke, or sliuchan, was also eaten in quantity, very often served with potatoes, or chewed raw. (In Japan, 250,000 tons of this seaweed are specially cultured annually.)

Dulse is a feathery seaweed cut from the rocks at lowtide. Wash it thoroughly in lots of running water to eliminate all sand, etc. Put in a heavy-bottomed saucepan with a little milk, a knob of butter, salt and pepper. Stew for 3–4 hours until really tender.
Serve with hot buttered oatcakes.

Spiced Beetroot Pickle

1.75 kg (4 lb) beetroot
1 teaspoon cloves
1 teaspoon peppercorns
1 teaspoon mustard seed
600 ml (1 pint) cider vinegar
1 tablespoon salt
225 g (8 oz) sugar

Cook the beetroot in boiling salted water until the skins slip off easily. Meanwhile simmer the spices in vinegar, salt and sugar for about half an hour. Then peel the beetroot and cut into slices or dice. Pack into jars. Cover with boiling spiced vinegar. Seal. *Makes about 6 one-pound jars.*

Sweet and Sour Beetroot

75 g (3 oz) sugar
1 level tablespoon cornflour
salt and pepper
150 ml (¼ pint) cider vinegar
2–3 cupfuls diced cooked beetroot
25 g (1 oz) butter

Who thinks 'sweet and sour' dishes are not Irish? Well, the ample proof that meats and fish were basted with honey while being grilled surely proves that the Irish palate always appreciated sweet and sour flavours. Who knows but the Chinese have borrowed the technique from us!

Blend the sugar, cornflour, seasoning and vinegar. Cook gently until clear. Add the beetroot and continue cooking for 10 minutes more. Stir in the butter just before serving. *Serves 3–4.*

Pickled Red Cabbage

1 large head of red cabbage
225 g (½ lb) salt
1.2 litres (2 pints) vinegar
12 g (½ oz) mace
12 g (½ oz) whole allspice
12 g (½ oz) cloves
6 peppercorns
12 g (½ oz) mustard seeds
12 g root ginger

Red cabbage is the richest flavoured of the cabbage tribe and is the traditional accompaniment to Irish Stew. It is also good with Irish spiced beef.

Traditional pickling takes three days ideally. On the first day shred the cabbage. Cover it lightly with salt. Leave it for two or three days, turning regularly. Next day, prepare the spiced vinegar. To make spiced vinegar, put the vinegar in a pan with the mace, allspice, cloves, peppercorns, mustard seed and root ginger. Bring to the boil. Remove from the fire and leave, covered, for about 24 hours to bring out and blend all the flavours together. On about the third day, shake off all possible salt – but don't wash the cabbage. Pack into jars. Cover with spiced vinegar. Cover. The spiced cabbage will be ready in about a fortnight. *Illustrated in colour on page 61.*

Creamy Onions

4–6 medium onions, peeled
½ teaspoon sugar
600 ml (1 pint) chicken stock
25 g (1 oz) flour
25 g (1 oz) butter
6 tablespoons fresh cream
salt and pepper
1 tablespoon parsley, chopped

There is, in every cook's opinion
No savoury dish without an onion
But lest your kissing should be spoilt
The onion must be thoroughly boiled.
(Dean Swift)

Peel the onions. Boil whole, with the sugar, in the stock for 10–15 minutes. In a heavy-bottomed pan, melt the butter. Blend in the flour and cook gently for 4 minutes. Add the stock very slowly, stirring

·CREAMY ONIONS·

½ small horseradish root
150 ml (¼ pint) vinegar
25 g (1 oz) sugar
450 g (1 lb) good eating apples
15 ml (1 tablespoon) olive oil
salt and pepper

2–3 parsnips
225 g (8 oz) streaky rashers

225 g (8 oz) raw potatoes, peeled
  and grated
225 g (8 oz) cooked, mashed
  potatoes
225 g (8 oz) flour
1 teaspoon baking powder
1 teaspoon salt
2 eggs, lightly beaten
75 ml (¼ cup) milk (approximately)

vigorously all the time to avoid lumps. Bring to the boil, lower the heat and cook for a further 15 minutes. Blend in the cream. Add salt and pepper to taste. Pour over the onions, sprinkle with chopped parsley and serve. *Serves 3–4.*

Horseradish and Apple Salad

Wash, peel and grate the horseradish and mix it at once with the vinegar and the sugar. Peel, core and thinly slice the apples. Pour the oil over the slices and sprinkle with salt and pepper. Mix with the horseradish. Serve with cold beef. *Serves 4.*

Parsnips and Rashers

Peel the parsnips and cut into 1 cm (¼ inch) thick rounds. Boil in salted water for 15–20 minutes or until tender but not mushy. Drain. Fry the rashers until crisp and much of the fat has drained into the pan. Remove the rashers from the pan and keep in a warm serving dish. Fry the rounds of parsnip for a few minutes in the rasher fat. Serve immediately with the rashers and potatoes in their jackets. *Serves 3–4.*

Boxty-on-the-griddle

Boxty, or rasp as it is sometimes called, was associated with the Great Famine, when people tried to eke out their limited supplies of potato. Its importance may be guessed from this old verse.

> *Boxty on the griddle*
> *Boxty on the pan*
> *If ye can't make boxty*
> *Ye'll never get a man.*

This is a County Cavan recipe.

Combine all the ingredients together, adding more milk if necessary to make a good dropping batter. Grease a heavy pan and drop the mixture by spoonfuls on the hot pan. Cook about 4 minutes on each side, until well cooked and brown.

Serve piping hot with lots of butter and, perhaps, honey. *Makes about 8–10 cakes.*

Buttered Parsnip and Carrot

1 medium parsnip
2 medium carrots
salt and pepper
25 g (1 oz) butter

Peel the parsnip and cut it into 1 cm ($\frac{1}{4}$ inch) thick rounds. Put to boil in salted water. Cut the carrots into 1 cm ($\frac{1}{4}$ inch) rounds. Allow the parsnip to boil for about 5 minutes, then add the carrot rounds. Cook for a further 15 minutes, or until just tender. Drain, then chop the carrots and parsnip together. Check the seasoning and toss with a generous knob of butter. *Serves 4.*

Mushroom Boxty

10 mushrooms
1 egg
salt and pepper
1 large potato, peeled
150 ml ($\frac{1}{4}$ pint) milk
25 g (1 oz) butter
nutmeg
25 g (1 oz) grated cheese

A north of Ireland song from the days of Bonnie Prince Charlie,

I'll have none of your boxty,
I'll have none of your blarney,
But I'll throw my petticoats over my head
And be off with my royal Charlie

immortalizes boxty.

'MUSHROOM BOXTY'.

Chop the mushrooms finely. Beat the egg and the salt and pepper. Grate the raw potato. Mix the potato and mushroom with the beaten egg and the butter. Add just enough milk to make the mixture soft. Form the mixture into thin little cakes and fry in butter. Serve them immediately, with roast chicken, or as a main course with a green salad. *Makes about 6 cakes.*

For variety, they may be arranged in an oven-proof dish, sprinkled with a little nutmeg and grated cheese, and browned in a hot oven.

Colcannon

6 large potatoes, peeled and boiled
6 spring onions, scallions or chives
150 ml ($\frac{1}{4}$ pint) milk or cream
salt and pepper
225 g (8 oz) boiled green curly kale
    or leaf cabbage
50 g (2 oz) butter
1 tablespoon chopped parsley

This is probably one of the oldest dishes in Ireland. It gets its name from three Gaelic words: *cal* (meaning kale) and *ceann fionn* (meaning white-headed) which well describe this tasty mixture of deep green kale and snowy white mashed potatoes. This is one of the handiest and most appetising ways I know of serving 'instant' potatoes.

Mash the potatoes finely and then chop the spring onions and add to the milk with salt and pepper. Bring to the boil. Chop the kale very finely and toss

70

in half of the butter. Fold the mashed potato, boiling milk and finely chopped kale together. Beat well until light and fluffy. Correct the seasoning. Serve immediately, piping hot and piled up on a serving dish, topped with the chopped parsley and the remainder of the butter. *Serves 6–8.*

Champ

¾ kg (½ lb) freshly cooked and mashed potatoes
bunch of spring onions, chopped
100 ml (4 fl oz) milk
salt and pepper
50g (2 oz) melted butter, or more

Keep the freshly mashed potatoes hot while softening the spring onions (green tops as well as white stalks) in the milk over a moderate heat. Then drain, reserving the milk.

Season the potatoes well and add the spring onions and enough hot milk to make a smooth, creamy mixture. Transfer to a warmed dish, make a hole in the center and pour the melted butter into it. Make sure everyone gets a good helping from the well of butter when serving. *Serves 4.*

Watercress Salad

4 bunches watercress
1 small head of lettuce
1 clove garlic
3 tablespoons olive oil
salt and freshly ground pepper
1 teaspoon lemon juice

Wash and dry watercress thoroughly. Trim off stalks. Wash and dry lettuce and tear into small pieces. Rub salad bowl with sliced garlic clove. Add lettuce and watercress. Combine oil, lemon juice and salt. Pour over salad and toss just before serving.

Buttered Salsify

450 g (1 lb) salsify
50 g (2 oz) butter
½ lemon
chives and dill

Salsify seems to have reached Ireland from Russia sometime during the reign of Henry VIII.

Peel the salsify under lots of running water and chop into even lengths. Sauté in butter over a low heat until tender. Add finely chopped herbs and lemon juice. Serve immediately. *Serves 3–4.*

Mock Oysters

a little lemon juice
450 g (1 lb) salsify, peeled and chopped

Salsify has a subtle fishy taste not unlike oysters, which inspired this very old dish.

3 eggs
salt and pepper
50 g (2 oz) butter

Cook the salsify in boiling salted water to which you have added a little lemon juice – this prevents the white salsify flesh from discolouring.

Chop and sieve the salsify. Beat the eggs thoroughly and mix them with the sieved salsify. Season well. Heat the butter in a pan. Pour oyster-sized spoonfuls of the mixture on the pan and fry until brown. Serve very hot with baked tomatoes. *Serves 3–4.*

1 kg (2 lbs) salsify

For the batter
100 g (4 oz) flour
1 teaspoon baking powder
1 egg
1 tablespoon oil
150 ml ($\frac{1}{4}$ pint) water
$\frac{1}{2}$ teaspoon mixed dried herbs

Salsify Fritters

Cook and peel the salsify, and cut into pieces about $2\frac{1}{2}$ cm (1 inch) long. Dip in the batter and fry in deep oil until crisp and golden. Drain and serve at once, with fried parsley and lemon wedges. *Serves 4–6.*

450 g (1 lb) parsnips
450 g (1 lb) swede turnips
50 g (2 oz) butter
salt
freshly ground pepper

Purée of Parsnips and Turnips

Peel parsnips and turnips thickly. Slice as thinly as you can, or put through a shredder. Plunge into boiling salted water and boil until just tender, for a minute or two depending on the thickness of the vegetable pieces. Drain well, then mash with a fork or sieve. Add butter, salt and freshly ground black pepper. *Serves 3–4.*

450 g (1 lb) potato
450 g (1 lb) celeriac
salt and white pepper
butter

Potato and Celeriac Purée

Peel and boil the potato and celeriac seperately, cutting the latter into manageable-sized pieces before cooking them. Then mash together and heat in a pan, seasoning to taste with salt and pepper and enriching with a huge lump of butter. *Serves 4–6.*

Excellent with all kinds of game.

Braised Vegetable Marrow

450 g (1 lb) vegetable marrow
50 g (2 oz) butter
salt and pepper
cayenne pepper

Peel the vegetable marrow. Remove and discard all seeds. Cut the flesh into bite-sized chunks. Melt the butter in a lidded casserole. Add marrow chunks, lots of salt, pepper and cayenne pepper. Cook in a lidded casserole in a moderate oven (350°F, Gas 4, 180°C) for $\frac{1}{2}$–$\frac{3}{4}$ hour. This delicious vegetable can be served straight from the oven – the marrow juice makes an excellent sauce. *Serves 3–4.*

Wicklow Chanterelle Omelet

The rich egg-yellow, apricot-scented chanterelles are just as much at home in the Wicklow forests as they are in the pine-clad Landes of France. Someone once said they were so delicious that they would bring dead men back to life!

225 g (8 oz) chanterelles
a little milk
3 eggs
salt and pepper
a knob of butter

Chanterelles are slightly tougher than other fungi and are best stewed in milk for about 10 minutes. Drain. Whisk the eggs and season with salt and pepper. Put a knob of butter in a pan and wait until it begins to foam and turn slightly brown. (The hot butter gives the omelet a nice nutty flavour as well as an appetizing golden colour.) Mix the pre-cooked chanterelles with the eggs and pour on to the foaming butter. Stir rapidly so that all the egg heats through. Leave for a minute or so, then fold over in half and serve immediately. *Serves 2.*

Cill Dara Ceps and Shallots

450 g (1 lb) fresh ceps
25 g (1 oz) butter
sea salt and freshly ground pepper
1 tablespoon chopped shallots or
    onion

The dense oak forests of Kildare (*Cill Dara*) are a happy hunting ground for ceps, blewits and lots of other delicious mushrooms in late summer and early autumn.

1 tablespoon breadcrumbs
squeeze of lemon juice
1 tablespoon chopped parsley

Wipe the ceps, slice the heads and chop the stalks. Heat butter in a pan. Add ceps and salt and pepper. Cook for a few minutes until they begin to brown. Then add the shallots and breadcrumbs. Fry all together for another few minutes. Before serving add lemon juice and sprinkle with chopped parsley. *Serves 4.*

Country Style Mushrooms

450 g (1 lb) mushrooms
50 g (2 oz) butter
salt and pepper
the juice of half a lemon
6 slices of hot toast

Wipe and slice the mushrooms. Melt the butter in a pan and sauté the mushrooms until well coloured. Salt and pepper and sprinkle with the lemon juice.

Serve as a delicious hot snack on squares of toast or, if you don't have to worry about your figure, on bread fried in the pan juices with a little extra butter added. *Serves 6.*

Creamy Vermouth Lawyer's Wig

225 g (8 oz) mushrooms, sliced
50 g (2 oz) butter
25 g (1 oz) flour
75 ml (5 tablespoons) fresh cream
salt and pepper
vermouth

This is an excellent way to prepare Lawyer's Wig mushrooms which are to be found in abundance almost everywhere – in pastures, roadsides, woodland – in late summer and until the first frosts.

Stew mushrooms in the butter in a lidded pan for about 20 minutes. Sprinkle with flour, stirring well with a wooden spoon. Add cream and simmer for 10 minutes. Pour in one tablespoon vermouth. Mix well.

Serve on toast, or in a tart. *Serves 4.*

Eggs Stuffed with Mushrooms

6 hard-boiled eggs
225 g (8 oz) mushrooms
300 ml (½ pint) white sauce
50 g (2 oz) grated Irish Cheddar
   cheese

'An egg is always an adventure.'
(Oscar Wilde)
'An egg without salt is like a kiss from a beardless man.'
(Proverb)

Shell the eggs and cut in half lengthwise. Remove the yolks and chop them finely with the mushrooms. Mix with a few spoonfuls of rich white sauce. Fill the egg-whites with this mixture. Arrange the stuffed eggs in an ovenproof dish and cover with a thin layer of white sauce. Sprinkle with grated cheese and brown slightly in a slow oven (300°F, Gas 2, 150°C). *Serves 3–4.*

Soyer's Mushroom and Kidney Sandwich

Alexis Soyer, Head Cook of All Ireland, in keeping with his brief: 'maximum food, minimum cost and maximum nutrition' devised this ingenious sandwich.

8 large mushrooms
50 g (2 oz) butter, melted
salt and pepper
4 lamb's kidneys, sliced
4 pieces of buttered toast

Brush the mushrooms with the melted butter, season and grill. Fry the kidneys in a little butter. Lay four mushrooms, black sides up, on to the toasts. Place the kidney slices on top of the mushrooms. Place the remaining mushrooms over the kidneys, black side down, to form a sandwich. Serve immediately. *Serves 4.*

· C O U N T R Y   S T Y L E
M U S H R O O M S ·

Sorrel-stuffed Turnips

Use small-to-medium, well-shaped young turnips for this dish, and peel them to make the contours even and round. With a sharp, pointed knife, cut a deep circle in the bottom of each – this will ensure that the turnips cook more quickly. Next, blanch them in boiling water until they are almost tender. Then drain and hollow out their centres.

Meanwhile cook and drain some sorrel (or spinach — in either case allowing about 100 g (4 oz) for each turnip). Then chop it, not too finely, and blend with enough thick double cream to make a smooth mixture.

Fill the turnips with this mixture, mounding it up in the centre; cut a slice off the bottom of each to help them stand upright, and finish the cooking in a deep sauté pan, in a good layer of butter over a gentle heat. Spoon the butter over the turnips before bringing to the table.

Turnips Kavanagh Style

1 medium swede turnip
100 g (4 oz) streaky rashers
salt and pepper

I am indebted to Dr Peter Kavanagh for this recipe for turnips as they were cooked in Inishkea and Monaghan when he was growing up there.

75

Peel and slice the turnip thickly. Boil in lots of salted water until the turnip is just tender – the cooking time will depend on the age of the turnip as well as on the thickness of the slices. Meanwhile fry the rashers in the pan. Remove when cooked and keep warm. Drain the turnip, put into the bacon fat and fry for a few minutes on either side. Add salt and pepper to taste and serve immediately with the rashers. *Serves 3–4.*

Peppery Turnips

1 medium swede turnip
1 bacon bone (optional)
pepper and salt
a large knob of butter

Turnips like a cold damp climate and have for long been an important part of the Irish diet.

Peel the turnip thickly and slice evenly. Put into a pan of boiling water and boil rapidly for 10–15 minutes until the turnip is tender but still has 'bite'. Drain and chop finely. Add lots of pepper and salt and toss in butter before serving. *Serves 3–4.*

Apple Sauce

225 g (½ lb) cooking apples
pinch of nutmeg
few tablespoons sugar
25 g (1 oz) butter

Peel, core and slice the apples then put them into a saucepan with the nutmeg and sugar and a little water. Cover and cook very gently over low heat until soft. Then sieve or beat with an electric mixer until smooth. Blend in the butter, and serve hot in a sauceboat.

Apple sauce is a traditional accompaniment to roast pork and goose.

Celery Stuffing

1 head celery
milk
100 g (4 oz) hazelnuts
75 g (3 oz) butter
175 g (6 oz) breadcrumbs
salt, pepper and nutmeg
1 clove garlic, crushed

This stuffing is excellent with roast turkey or chicken

Wash and chop celery and cook in a little milk until tender. Blanch and roast the nuts in a little butter. Mix with the breadcrumbs. Mix all the ingredients together, including the celery and its cooking liquid, to make a soft, moist stuffing. Add the seasoning, garlic and, if needed, a little more milk to bind.

76

BAKING

One of the great traditions of Irish cooking is surely its baking – the delicious crusty cakes of soda and wheaten bread still baked in so many Irish homes – arguably the best bread in the world.

Bread was sometimes baked in a primitive oven wrapped in cabbage leaves, later – and indeed until modern times – in a bastable oven, a heavy cast-iron pot with a hollow lid which sat right into the open hearth. The lid was hollow to accommodate the glowing peat sods that ensured even cooking of the bread on all sides. It was a technique which took skill and long years of experience to perfect! The other method was using the griddle – a heavy, flat-bottomed pan. Dough was kneaded, rolled out fairly thinly and cut into triangles or farls. These were then cooked first on one side, then on the other and often eaten immediately, steaming hot and dripping with lots of butter. Oaten cakes seem to have an even more venerable ancestry than soda bread. As early as the twelfth century, oats seem to have been the main cereal crop in the land and emigrants heading off across the globe often carried a supply of Mother's oat-cakes in their kerchiefs. Strange to say, though yeast was used generously in ale-making, traditional Irish baking used it rarely, preferring soured milk or that great stand-by, buttermilk.

Cows in rural Ireland were milked twice a day, the rich cream skimmed off and added to the earthenware crock standing on the dairy floor. When the cream was ripe, it was tipped into the huge revolving churn. The churn was firmly lidded, for it revolved fairly quickly. The cream was salted and scalded and in no time at all the rich yellow country butter was made. The liquid left in the churn when the butter was removed was buttermilk. Fresh buttermilk was regarded as second to none as a sharp, tart thirst-quencher. It was also used to bake bread. Lent, however, was regarded as a most important time in the ancient Irish calendar; a time of 'black fast'. Not only was flesh meat strictly forbidden, but dairy products, milk, eggs and cheese were equally taboo. (Strange to say an exception was made for the Barnacle Goose which, because of its fishy taste, some strange casuistry passed for eating by the faithful during Lent.) Anyhow, come Lent with its total ban on meats and milk, how was the woman of the house to bake her bread? At this time of the year, she substituted yeast or *bairm* for buttermilk. Some, however, had neither the skill nor the equipment to use the yeast and they existed on unleavened bread for the duration of Lent.

· RICH PLUM PUDDING

Bairm Breac

150 ml (¼ pint) tepid milk
25 g (1 oz) sugar
12 g (½ oz) yeast
225 g (8 oz) plain flour
pinch of salt
75 g (3 oz) sultanas
25 g (1 oz) butter

Traditionally, *bairm* or yeast was only used as leaven during the Black Fast of Lent when all meats and dairy produce were forbidden – including the buttermilk normally used in bread-making. *Breac* is a Gaelic word meaning spotted and refers to the peel, currants etc, in the cake.

Mix the milk, sugar and yeast together. Sieve the flour and salt together. Make a well in the centre. Add the milk, sugar and yeast. Mix into a soft dough. Beat with a wooden spoon for 5 minutes. Next, mix in the cleaned fruit and peel. Put into a greased tin. Leave to rise in a warm place for about 1½ hours. The mixture should rise to double its size.
 Bake in a hot oven (425°F, Gas 7, 220°C) for about 25 minutes.

A Rich Plum Pudding

350 g (12 oz) butter
350 g (12 oz) brown sugar
5 eggs
700 g (1½ lb) breadcrumbs
1 kg (2¼ lb) raisins and sultanas, mixed
25 g (1 oz) mixed spice
50 g (2 oz) ground almonds
25 g (1 oz) chopped almonds
1 cooking apple, peeled and grated
rind and juice of 1 lemon
50 g (2 oz) mixed peel
½ tablespoon golden syrup
¼ tablespoon coffee essence
½ teaspoon bread soda
½ bottle Guinness
¾ glass brandy

This recipe, given to me by Mrs Egan from Athlone, differs from the old traditional recipes in that it uses neither flour nor suet and therefore, though really rich, is lighter and more in keeping with modern tastes.

Cream the butter and the sugar. Beat the eggs and add, one at a time, to the creamed butter. Stir in the breadcrumbs, raisins, sultanas, spices, almonds, apple, lemon and mixed peel, golden syrup, coffee essence and bread soda. Mix with the Guinness and the brandy.
 Put the mixture into 900 g (2 lb) bowls – there should be enough for four puddings. Cover with foil and steam for 6 hours.
 Serve flaming with Irish whiskey.

Boiled Cake

225 g (8 oz) butter
450 g (1 lb) raisins
225 g (8 oz) brown sugar
450 ml (¾ pint) fresh milk
1 level teaspoon each of nutmeg, cinnamon and mixed spice
4 large eggs

This is a West Clare traditional recipe from Mrs Keating of Ciosa, Kilkee.

Put the butter, raisins, brown sugar, milk and spices in a heavy saucepan. Bring to the boil, then simmer for about 10 minutes. Allow to cool.

350 g (12 oz) plain flour
½ teaspoon baking powder
½ teaspoon bread soda
50 g (2 oz) mixed peel

When cool, add the beaten eggs, flour, baking powder, bread soda and mixed peel. Stir well until all the ingredients are well mixed. The mixture may seem sloppy, but there is no need to add extra flour.

Bake in a lined cake tin for 1½ hours in a moderate oven (350°F, Gas 4, 180°C).

Richmond Cake

75 g (3 oz) margarine
225 g (8 oz) plain flour
100 g (4 oz) sugar
100 g (4 oz) currants
½ teaspoon baking powder
pinch of salt
2 eggs, beaten
150 ml (¼ pint) milk
(approximately)

Rub the margarine into the flour, then add all the dry ingredients. Mix to a stiff paste with the beaten eggs and a little milk. Bake in a flat, greased tin in a moderately hot oven (400°F, Gas 6, 200°C) for about ½ hour.

Mr Guinness Cake

225 g (8 oz) butter
225 g (8 oz) brown sugar
4 eggs, lightly beaten
275 g (10 oz) plain flour
2 level teaspoons mixed spices
225 g (8 oz) seedless raisins
225 g (8 oz) sultanas
100 g (4 oz) mixed peel
100 g (4 oz) walnuts, chopped
8–12 tablespoons Guinness

Cream butter and sugar together until light and creamy. Gradually beat in the eggs. Sieve flour and mixed spices together and fold in with the eggs. Add the raisins, sultanas, mixed peel and walnuts. Mix well together. Stir 4 tablespoons of Guinness into the mixture and mix to a soft dropping consistency. Turn into a prepared 18 cm (7 inch) round cake tin and bake in a very moderate oven (325°F, Gas 3, 160°C) for 1 hour. Then reduce the heat to a cool oven (300°F, Gas 2, 150°C) and cook for another 1½ hours. Allow to become cold before removing from cake tin. Prick the base of the cake with a skewer and spoon over the remaining 4–8 tablespoons of Guinness. Keep cake for one week before eating.

Rossylongan Cake

450 g (1 lb) flour
225 g (8 oz) butter
225 g (8 oz) currants
225 g (8 oz) raisins
100 g (4 oz) mixed peel
2 teaspoons mixed spice
350 g (12 oz) brown sugar
grated rind of one lemon
1 teaspoon bread soda
1 bottle Guinness
4 eggs

Sieve the flour and rub in the butter. Add the cleaned fruit, peel, spice and sugar. Heat the Guinness, pour it over the soda in a bowl; beat the eggs, then add them and the Guinness to the flour, fat and fruit mixture. Stir well and beat for 15 minutes. Bake in a slow oven (300°F, Gas 2, 150°C) for 3 hours.

Keep for at least a week before cutting.

Castleconnell Cake

50 g (2 oz) butter or margarine
350 g (12 oz) flour
1 teaspoon baking powder
175 g (6 oz) caster sugar
50 g (2 oz) candied peel
225 g (8 oz) currants
100 g (4 oz) sultanas
1 teaspoon mixed spice
3 eggs, separated
a little milk

Rub the butter or margarine and baking powder together. Add the rest of the dry ingredients. Separate the egg whites from the yolks. Add a little milk to the yolks and stir into the mixture. Whisk the whites until they are stiff. Fold in lightly. Turn the mixture out into a well-greased and lined 25.4 cm (10 inch) tin and bake in a moderate oven (350°F, Gas 4, 180°C) for about $1\frac{1}{2}$ hours.

Apple Cake (traditional)

For the pastry
150 g (5 oz) plain flour
75 g (3 oz) cornflour
pinch of baking powder
2 egg yolks
100 g (4 oz) sugar
grated peel of $\frac{1}{2}$ lemon
a few drops of vanilla flavouring
75 g (3 oz) chilled butter

For the filling
450 g (1 lb) cooking apples
35 g ($1\frac{1}{2}$ oz) raisins
25 g (1 oz) sugar

Sieve together the flour, cornflour and baking powder. Make a well in the centre and mix in the egg yolks, sugar, lemon peel and vanilla. Take the butter from the refrigerator and flake it on to the mixture with a sharp knife. Quickly work all the ingredients together.

Refrigerate for $\frac{1}{2}$ hour. Roll out lightly and line a greased 20 cm (8 inch) tin. Prick the bottom over with a fork. Peel and core the apples and slice thinly on to the pastry, sprinkling with the raisins and a little sugar.

Bake in a hot oven (425°F, Gas 7, 220°C) for 40–45 minutes. *Serves 4–6.*

Saffron Cake

12 g ($\frac{1}{2}$ oz) yeast
150 ml ($\frac{1}{4}$ pint) warm water
25 g (1 oz) sugar
225 g (8 oz) plain flour
pinch of salt
100 g (4 oz) butter
1 egg, beaten
a pinch of saffron
75 g (3 oz) seedless raisins
25 g (1 oz) candied peel

Surprisingly, vast quantities of saffron were imported into Ireland in the nineteenth century. I couldn't track down any traditional recipes using it, but it was probably used in baking, for medicinal purposes, and mainly as a dye for fabrics.

Stir the yeast and sugar into the warm water and mix with part of the flour to make a soft dough. Cover with a cloth and leave in a warm place to rise (it should more or less double in size). Sift the remaining flour into a basin with the salt. Cream the butter and the remainder of the sugar. Add the beaten egg. Infuse the saffron in a little warm water. Combine with the yeast dough. Knead with the raisins and the peel. Put into a greased 25.4 cm (10 inch) baking tin and leave to rise again. Put into a moderate oven (350°F, Gas 4, 180°C) and bake for 1–$1\frac{1}{2}$ hours.

Hazel Cottage Cheesecake

75 g (3 oz) butter
25 g (1 oz) sugar
3 eggs, separated
75 g (3 oz) cottage cheese
75 g (3 oz) roasted hazelnuts,
    chopped
25 g (1 oz) breadcrumbs
jam, nuts and grated chocolate to
    decorate

Cream the butter and sugar together. Add the egg yolks, mix the cottage cheese and chopped hazelnuts. Whisk the egg whites until stiff. Fold the breadcrumbs and then the egg whites into the mixture.

Pile into a well-greased cake-tin and bake in a moderate oven (350°F, Gas 4, 180°C) for about 40 minutes.

Spread a little jam on the cake and decorate with nuts and grated chocolate.

Hazelnut Tart

6 eggs
225 g (8 oz) sugar
350 g (12 oz) grated hazelnuts
25 g (1 oz) flour
1 tablespoon rum
$\frac{1}{4}$ teaspoon grated lemon peel

For the filling and topping
raspberry jam
whipped cream
icing sugar
chopped nuts

Separate the egg yolks from the whites. Beat the yolks and sugar together until creamy. Mix the nuts with egg yolks and sugar. Beat the egg whites until stiff. Fold in the egg whites and flour. Add the rum and lemon peel and mix until smooth. Pile the mixture into a 30.5 cm (12 inch) cake-tin and bake in a moderate oven (350°F, Gas 4, 180°C) for 40–45 minutes. When cold, split in half and spread the bottom half with raspberry jam and cream. Dredge with icing sugar and decorate with a few chopped nuts.

Gooseberry Tartlets

350 g (12 oz) plain flour
$\frac{1}{4}$ teaspoon salt
100 g (4 oz) butter
100 g (4 oz) sugar
1 egg, beaten
1 teaspoon vanilla essence
1 tablespoon cream

For the gooseberry curd
2 egg yolks
1 cup stewed gooseberries

This recipe was invented by Emily, first Duchess of Leinster, for her favourite son, Lord Edward Fitzgerald – who, unfortunately, was later executed in the Tower of London.

Sift the flour and salt together. Cream the butter and sugar. Add the beaten egg, vanilla essence and cream. Gradually, mix in the flour. Leave in the refrigerator for an hour or so. Roll out to 0.3 cm ($\frac{1}{8}$ inch) thick.

Make the gooseberry curd by mixing 2 egg yolks with the stewed, sieved, sweetened gooseberries.

Line patty tins with the dough. Fill with gooseberry curd. Cover with pastry lids and bake for 15 minutes in a moderate oven (375°F, Gas Mark 5, 190°C).

Rutland Crumpets

225 g (8 oz) plain flour
pinch of salt
12 g (½ oz) sugar
1 egg, beaten
300 ml (½ pint) buttermilk
pinch of bread soda

· R V T L A N D
C R V M P E T S ·

These crumpets were traditionally cooked on the griddle but may also be baked.

Put the flour, salt and sugar in a bowl. Make a well in the centre and put in the beaten egg. Add a little buttermilk, stirring with a wooden spoon. Beat well to get the mixture smooth and free of lumps. Add the rest of the buttermilk. Blend the bread soda in a little buttermilk and add it to the mixture last thing before cooking.

To griddle
Use a heavy-bottomed pan. Heat thoroughly. Rub over with a small piece of dripping or lard. Spoon the batter on to the heated griddle. Pour on as many spoonfuls as the pan will hold. Cook until a light brown on one side. Turn and cook through. Butter them, put two crumpets together and serve really hot with honey poured over – a real treat for afternoon tea.

Flapjacks

175 g (6 oz) butter
175 g (6 oz) brown sugar
225 g (8 oz) rolled oats
a pinch of salt

Melt the butter in a saucepan over a gentle heat. Mix in the sugar, oats and salt. Stir well and turn the mixture on to a greased baking sheet and press lightly together. Smooth with a knife.
  Bake in a moderate oven (350°F, Gas 4, 180°C) for 30–40 minutes, then cut across into squares or fingers. Leave on the baking sheet until quite cold.

Kildare Scones

225 g (8 oz) plain flour
½ teaspoon baking powder
1 teaspoon sugar
25 g (1 oz) butter
150 ml (¼ pint) milk

Sift the flour and baking powder together. Mix in the sugar. Cut the butter into the mixture and keep cutting until the mixture looks like fine bread-crumbs. Moisten with milk to make a soft dough. Turn the dough out on to a lightly floured board and knead lightly and quickly about 6 times. Roll out to 1.2 cm (½ inch) thick and cut into scones using a floured cutter or knife. Bake in a hot oven (450°F, Gas 8, 230°C) for 10 minutes.
  Cut in two and butter while very hot. Serve on a folded napkin.

83

Griddle Scones

350 g (12 oz) plain flour
1 teaspoon baking powder
25 g (1 oz) caster sugar
½ teaspoon salt
2 eggs, well beaten
450 ml (¾ pint) milk
50 g (2 oz) butter, melted

Invest in a heavy iron frying pan or griddle and you will be able to make these scones in next to no time – and you don't even need an oven.

Sift the dry ingredients together. Combine the well-beaten eggs with the milk. Add to the flour and beat the mixture until smooth. Add the melted butter.

Rub the pan with fat – avoid over-greasing – and heat it thoroughly. Pour the batter on the griddle with a large spoon. When bubbles appear on the surface, the cakes are ready for turning. Cook over a moderate heat for about 2½–3 minutes on each side. Serve piping hot with lots of honey or spread with butter. If the batter is stored in a refrigerator for about 24 hours before cooking, the scones will be even lighter.

Soda Bread

450 g (1 lb) plain flour
1 teaspoon salt
1 teaspoon sugar
1 teaspoon bread soda
400 ml (⅔ pint) buttermilk

Everybody knows that Soda Bread is the traditional bread of Ireland. If you don't churn, the recipe below will explain how to make buttermilk very simply without churning.

Sift the flour, salt, sugar and bread soda together a few times to mix them thoroughly. Make a well in the centre and stir in the buttermilk gradually to make a soft dough. Turn out on a floured board and knead lightly for a few minutes. Flatten it out to about 1.2 cms (½ inch) thick. With a floured knife, cut a cross on it to help it cook evenly throughout.

Bake at once in a hot oven (450°F, Gas 8, 230°C) for 45 minutes. (To test whether the cake is done or not, tap the bottom – if cooked it should sound hollow.)

Buttermilk without a churn or Buttermilk Plant

25 g (1 oz) sugar
25 g (1 oz) yeast
1.2 litres (2 pints) milk, tepid
1.2 litres (2 pints) water, tepid

All the experts agree that buttermilk makes the best bread, but if you don't churn there is no need to despair of having some of this excellent commodity

· BUTTERMILK ·

both for baking and as a really refreshing drink on a hot day. Here's how to literally grow your own buttermilk!

Mix the sugar and yeast together. Gradually add the tepid milk and water. Cover and leave at room temperature for 2 days. By then, it should have the sharp, pleasant smell of buttermilk. Strain the buttermilk and use it as usual. Keep the sponge-like residue that remains in the strainer. Rinse it thoroughly in tepid water, place in a scalded vessel, add more tepid milk and water and make more buttermilk.

Your buttermilk plant will go on producing buttermilk for ever, as long as you are careful to strain and wash it about every 5 days, and also remember always to have the water and milk mixture tepid – strong heat kills yeast.

Oatmeal Scones

100 g (4 oz) plain flour
½ teaspoon salt
1 teaspoon sugar
1 teaspoon baking powder
100 g (4 oz) fine oatmeal
50 g (2 oz) butter
150 ml (¼ pint) milk

Sift the flour, salt, sugar and baking powder together a few times. Mix in the oatmeal. Rub in the butter. Mix to a soft dough with the milk. Turn out on to a floured board and knead lightly. Divide the dough into two portions and knead into round cakes. Cut into quarters (the traditional _farls_) and place on a greased tin. Bake in a hot oven (425°F, Gas 7, 210°C) for 15 minutes.

Strones or Oatcakes

225 g (8 oz) oatmeal
a pinch of baking powder
a pinch of salt
1 teaspoon of bacon fat
boiling water

For hundreds of years in Ulster, a large _strone_ was made in the shape of a cross to celebrate the feast of St Brigit. Strones were traditionally served hot and dripping with freshly made butter. The butter was considered so important that the chronicler of the Annals of the Kingdom of Ireland in 1486 notes that 'Neidhe O'Mulconry, head of the inhospitality of Ireland, died. It was he who solemnly swore that he would never give bread and butter together to guests.'

Mix the dry ingredients – the oatmeal, baking powder, and salt. Melt the fat in a little boiling water and use to mix the other ingredients to a stiff

85

dough. Scatter lots of oatmeal on the board and turn the dough out on this. Scatter more oatmeal over it and knead thoroughly. Roll out as thinly as possible, in a circle. Put on a baking sheet. Cut a cross on top so that when cooked the oatcake can easily be broken into quarters, the traditional farls.

Bake in a moderate oven (350°F, Gas 4, 180°C) for about 20 minutes. Serve with lots of butter.

Oatmeal Bread

300 ml (½ pint) cooked porridge
(recipe below)
a few drops of vanilla essence
25 g (1 oz) margarine
1 tablespoon treacle or honey
1 teaspoon salt
12 g (½ oz) yeast
225 ml (⅜ pint) lukewarm water
and milk, mixed
700 g (1½ lb) wholemeal flour

Cook the porridge normally, adding a few drops of vanilla essence. Add the margarine, honey or treacle and salt. Put the flour in a basin. Make a well in the centre and add the porridge mixture. Soften the yeast in the tepid water and stir it into the porridge when it is lukewarm. Leave in a warm place overnight. Knead well next morning and allow the dough to stand for another hour. Grease two 450 g (1 lb) tins very thoroughly and bake in a moderate oven (350°F, Gas 4, 180°C) for about 40 minutes, or until the loaves are well risen, a good brown colour and shrinking a little from the sides of the tins.

Stirabout or Porridge

125 g (5 oz) oatmeal
900 ml (1½ pints) boiling water
½ teaspoon salt or sugar

Irish Stirabout has long been famed throughout the world. When St Jerome in the fourth century wanted to heap abuse on his enemy, Celestine, according to the legend, he called him 'a great fool of a man swelled out with Irish Stirabout'. Mac Conglinne, dreaming of the gastronomic delights of his country, saw a huge cauldron of stirabout, 'the treasure that is smoothest and sweetest of all foods'. According to the experts, the secret of good porridge-making is to add pinches of oatmeal as the porridge boils, so that the finished dish presents a complete gamut of taste and texture from mushy, fully boiled to almost raw meal.

Sprinkle the oatmeal into the boiling water, stirring all the time. Boil the mixture for a few minutes. Then cover with a lid and simmer gently for 15–30 minutes, depending on the condition of the oatmeal. 5 or 10 minutes before the end of cooking, add the salt. If it is added early on, it tends to harden the oatmeal.

'STIRABOUT.'

Fadge or Potato Cakes

225 g (8 oz) freshly boiled potatoes
½ teaspoon salt
25 g (1 oz) melted butter
25 g (1 oz) onion, very finely
    chopped
50 g (2 oz) plain flour
    (approximately)

Mash the freshly cooked potatoes. Add the salt, melted butter and onion. Using a minimum of flour, work the mixture into a dough. Roll out in a circular shape about 0.6 cm (¼ inch) thick. Cut into 6 or 8 farls and cook on a hot, slightly greased griddle until nicely browned on both sides.

Fadge is normally served really hot with lots of butter. Alternatively, the farls may be fried with bacon, puddings and sausages. *Serves 4–6.*

Wheaten Honey Cakes

225 g (8 oz) coarse-ground
    wheaten meal
1 egg
225 g (8 oz) honey
a pinch of salt
50 g (2 oz) melted butter

Bricriu in his legendary vision of the pleasures of the table dreams of 'five score cakes of wheat, cooked in honey'.

Put all the ingredients in a basin and beat well together. Lightly grease a griddle or heavy-bottomed pan. Drop the mixture in spoonfuls on to it and cook over a moderate heat until browned on both sides.

Wheaten Oat Biscuits

100 g (4 oz) margarine
100 g (4 oz) sugar
1 egg
100 g (4 oz) wholemeal
½ teaspoon salt
100 g (4 oz) rolled oats
½ teaspoon baking powder

Cream the margarine and the sugar together. Beat the egg and add to the creamed mixture. Mix all the dry ingredients together and combine with the creamed mixture. Turn out on to a well floured board. Roll out as thinly as possible and cut in fingers. Brush with the egg remaining in the beating bowl. Bake in a hot oven (425°F, Gas 7, 220°C) for 9–10 minutes.

Craebh or Gingerbread

1 egg
100 g (4 oz) brown sugar
225 g (8 oz) treacle
100 g (4 oz) butter
300 ml (½ pint) hot water
350 g (12 oz) plain flour
¼ teaspoon salt
1 teaspoon each ginger, cinnamon
    and bread soda

Midsummer celebrations revolved around the *craebh*, a small basket of gingerbread placed on a beribboned pole. The best musician played beneath the pole and the dancers vied with one another to win the *craebh*. This is the origin of the expression 'that takes the cake' (*bhain se an craebh leis* – he won).

Combine and mix well together the egg, the sugar and the treacle. In another bowl combine and beat the butter and the hot water together until the butter liquifies. Add the egg mixture and blend well together. Sift the flour, salt and spices and add to the mixture, beating just enough to blend the ingredients together. Pour the batter into a lightly greased tin and bake in a moderate oven (350°F, Gas 4, 180°C) for 50 minutes.

Honey Nut Loaf

100 g (4 oz) flour
225 g (8 oz) bran
½ teaspoon bread soda
½ teaspoon salt
25 g (1 oz) melted butter
100 g (4 oz) finely chopped nuts
100 g (4 oz) honey
450 ml (¾ pint) milk

Sieve the flour, bran, bread soda and salt together. Add the butter, finely chopped nuts and the honey. Mix to a soft dough with the milk. Bake in a well-greased tin for about 25 minutes in a hot oven (425°F, Gas 7, 220°C).

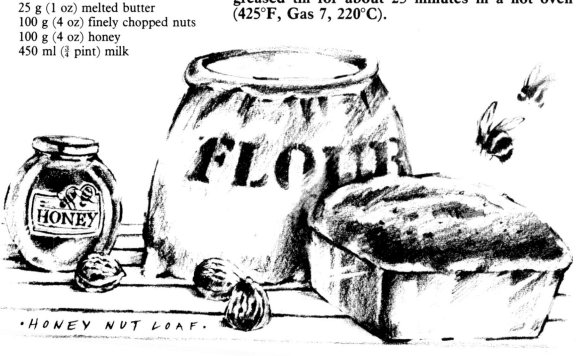

·HONEY NUT LOAF·

SWEETS AND SWEETIES

The Irish have always had a sweet tooth. Not surprisingly, honey has always been a great favourite. In the Brehon Laws, its importance was recognized in a special section dealing with bee-keeping and problems relating to the ownership of honey. Even in those early days, a clear distinction was made between domesticated and wild bees. By law, any man who found a swarm of bees was entitled to one quarter of the honey produced at the end of the year. Since bees gathered honey from the neighbours' farms, the neighbours were entitled to a small share of the honey. Meat and fish were basted with honey, and honey and milk were mixed to make a pleasant drink. *Metheglin*, a drink made in Ancient Ireland from honey, water and possibly herbs, was considered an ideal drink for women. As well, lard and honey were mixed and used as a condiment. On special occasions, they ate stirabout with honey. Vast quantities of honey, fermented, made the much appreciated alcoholic drink, mead.

Fresh fruit was also gathered and eaten with relish. The womenfolk collected fruits in the woods. In *Duanaire Finn* (Anthology of Old Irish Poetry, ed. Eoin Mac Neill, London 1908) we get an idea of what was available: 'Your woods afford a rich harvest to the fair women of the Fianna. Your berries, your small fruits and your blackberries formed a fragrant crop. Raspberries and strawberries, cress and sloes and woodbine – even your coarse fruit was plentiful in the time of the Fianna.' Again and again, apples (very often Armagh apples) were referred to in the most glowing terms: 'apple-treed Eamhain' [or Armagh], or 'Eamhain of the fragrant apple trees.' In *Duanaire Finn*, the hero declares: 'I will eat good apples in the glen, and fragrant berries of the rowan-tree.'

Apples were almost certainly brought by the Celts from Central Asia when they came to settle in Europe. Long after the Fianna were no more, the sweetie-shop at the street corner became a haven for sweet-toothed youngsters. Fruit jujubes, big slabs of irregularly broken treacly toffee, aniseed (called Nancy) balls, and gaudily coloured lollipops took the place of the honey and fruits of an earlier age.

Except for apple tarts, there seems to be no great tradition of pastry-making in the country. The Danes, at the time of their incursions into Ireland, hadn't perfected their own pastry-making skills and therefore they couldn't pass them on to the native Irish. However, cakes and puddings are part of the Irish way of life. Plum pudding, wrapped in a greased pudding cloth, was cooked for hours and hours in the farmhouse kitchen, filling the whole place with the most exciting aroma. Incidentally, plum pudding was originally a savoury meant to go with a fat goose. It contained plums, hence its name.

The hazel tree was revered in ancient Ireland – the penalty for anyone caught cutting one down was death. Hazelnuts were much appreciated.

· BANANAS À LA KRAPP ·

Sugared Oranges

3–4 oranges
4 tablespoons sugar

Peel and remove all the pith from the oranges. Separate the segments and lay them in a shallow dish. Squeeze the juice from half an orange and pour over the segments. Sprinkle sugar all over them. Place under a hot grill until the sugar browns and caramelizes. Serve immediately. *Serves 3–4.*

Bananas à la Krapp

4 small, well ripened bananas
4 tablespoons water
4 tablespoons honey
100 g (4 oz) hazelnuts, crushed
4 teaspoons Irish Mist

This recipe is dedicated to Mr Samuel Beckett, one of my favourite Irishmen.

Preheat the oven to 425°F, Gas 7, 220°C. Heat the honey, water and hazelnuts. Whisk the mixture lightly. Fold sheets of aluminium foil into 4 shallow boat shapes, each just large enough to hold a banana. Place a peeled banana in each and sprinkle it with the honey mixture and Irish Mist.

Fold up the edges of each boat to seal it completely and bake in a hot oven (425°F, Gas Mark 7, 220°C) for 20 minutes. When they are cooked, serve the foil parcels as they are to the guests – they can open them themselves.

Apple Snow

2 apples
1 egg white
sugar to taste

Bake the apples in a moderate oven (350°F, Gas 4, 180°C) until tender. Remove the pulp and beat until smooth. Whisk the egg until stiff and fold into the apple pulp. Sweeten to taste. *Serves 2.*

Baked Apples

4 large cooking apples
2 tablespoons honey
a few hazelnuts, chopped
100 g (4 oz) butter
whipped cream

Preheat the oven to 350°F, Gas 4, 180°C. Remove apple cores and slice the skins horizontally along the middle but do not peel. Put a little boiling water into a greased baking tin. Mix the honey, chopped hazelnuts and butter together and spoon the mixture into the apple centres. Bake in the oven for about 30 minutes, or until apples are tender. Serve hot or cold with whipped cream. *Serves 4.*

Jellied Apples

450 g (1 lb) apples
50 g (2 oz) sugar
strip of lemon rind or a few cloves
300 ml (½ pint) water
gelatine

Wipe, peel and slice the apples and put in a saucepan with the sugar, lemon rind and water. Stew until tender and rub through a sieve. Measure the purée. Allow 12 g (½ oz) gelatine to 600 ml (1 pint) of purée. Dissolve the gelatine in a little water and stir into the purée. When the mixture is cold, pour into a mould. When set, turn out. Serve with lots of whipped cream. *Serves 4.*

Fruit Fritters

Fruit according to season

Coating batter
100 g (4 oz) flour
25 g (1 oz) melted butter or oil
150 ml (¼ pint) milk
2 eggs

There's always an element of surprise about fritters – it's half their attraction. Then there is the contrast between the crisp, golden coat of batter on the outside and the soft sweetness of the inside. Apples, pears, oranges and strawberries are all well suited for fritters, or why not use a variety of fruit according to season?

Sieve the flour. Separate the eggs. Beat about half of the milk into the flour. Add the beaten egg yolks and melted butter or oil, and beat well. Continue adding milk until the batter is smooth and thin. Coating batter should be slightly thicker than pancake batter, just thick enough to coat the fritter completely but thinly. Leave the batter in a cool place for at least one hour. Just before using, whisk the egg whites stiffly and fold into the batter.
To fry the fritters
Fritters must be fried in deep fat. The pan should be filled not more than three-quarters full. The oil must be well heated, so that the fritter sets immediately. *Serves 4.*

·FRVIT FRITTERS·

Ashbourne Cheesecake

1 225 g (8 oz) tin of pineapple
12 g (½ oz) powdered gelatine
150 ml (¼ pint) double cream
juice and grated rind of 1 lemon
100 g (4 oz) caster sugar
2 eggs, separated
450 g (1 lb) Philadelphia cheese, beaten

This cheesecake is a speciality of Chris Garde's Ashbourne House Hotel in Co. Cork.

Drain the syrup from the pineapple. Sprinkle the gelatine on the syrup. Chop the pineapple finely. Whisk the cream until thick, and add the juice and rind of 1 lemon. Dissolve the gelatine in the syrup over a pan of hot water. Add the sugar and the

6 digestive biscuits
1 teaspoon sugar
37 g (1½ oz) butter

egg-yolks and heat gently until the mixture thickens. Let the mixture cool but not set. Add the beaten cheese. Whip the cream and stir in. Whisk the egg whites stiffly and fold into the mixture. Turn the mixture into a well-oiled baking tin and chill until set. To make the crust, crush the biscuits with a rolling pin and combine with the sugar and butter. Sprinkle over the cheesecake and press down lightly. Chill until firm. Unmould and decorate to taste. *Serves 6.*

Fruit Jujubes

450 g (1 lb) tinned apricots
350 g (12 oz) sugar
1 teaspoon almond essence

Strain the apricots and rub through a sieve. Put in a saucepan with the sugar. Bring slowly to the boil, stirring all the time. Continue to stir until the mixture is thick. Test a drop of the mixture (as when making jam) to see if it sets. When setting point is reached, allow to cool. Stir in the almond essence. Drop the mixture in teaspoonfuls on greased paper. When quite cold, toss in granulated sugar. Store in an airtight tin or jar.

Lollipops

150 ml (¼ pint) water
450 g (1 lb) sugar
olive oil
1 tablespoon glucose powder
yellow or red food colouring
lemon or strawberry flavouring

Put the water and the sugar into a saucepan and heat gently until the sugar has dissolved. Grease a baking sheet with oil. Add the glucose to the mixture and bring to the boil. Remove from the heat. Divide the mixture into two portions and add the desired colouring. Re-boil half the syrup until it will form a hard ball when dropped into cold water. Flavour with 4 or 5 drops of selected flavouring, then quickly drop spoonfuls on to the oiled baking sheet. Put a stick into each round. Leave to set hard. Repeat the process with the rest of the syrup. When all the lollipops are set and hard, wrap in cellophane.

Toffee Apple Sticks

450 g (1 lb) sugar
50 g (2 oz) butter
2 teaspoons vinegar
150 ml (¼ pint) water
1 tablespoon golden syrup
6 medium sized apples

Grease a deep baking tin. Put all the ingredients except the apples into a large heavy saucepan. Heat gently until dissolved, then boil rapidly for 5 minutes, stirring occasionally to prevent the mixture from sticking or burning. Test the syrup by dropping a little of it into cold water to see if it will form a hard ball; if it does not form a hard ball, continue boiling until it does.

Push wooden sticks into the apples, then dip them into the toffee. Twirl them around for a few seconds and then leave them to cool on a baking tray.

Fudge

50 g (2 oz) butter
450 g (1 lb) soft brown sugar
300 ml (½ pint) milk
4 drops vanilla essence

Put the butter, sugar and milk into a large, heavy saucepan and heat gently until the sugar has dissolved.

Grease a 20 × 12 cms (8 × 5 inch) baking tin with a little butter.

Bring the mixture to the boil, stirring constantly. Boil fast for about 15 minutes – but take care the mixture does not boil over. Test some in cold water to see if it forms a soft ball. If not, continue to boil until it does so. Add the vanilla essence. Remove from the heat and beat the mixture with a whisk until it thickens and feels tough. Pour into a greased tin and leave in a cool place to set. Mark into squares with a knife. Cut into squares.

Rosehip Syllabub

1 large lemon
½ bottle rosehip wine, or any dry wine
50 g (2 oz) caster sugar
300 ml (½ pint) double cream

Syllabub was, in bye-gone times, a countryman's favourite summer treat. Knee-deep in rich clover pastures, the cows produced an abundance of thick creamy milk. Syllabub was made to celebrate this bounty. An old recipe tells how: 'take your best china bowl, half fill it with wine, hold it under your favourite cow and squirt the rich milk directly into the wine to fill the bowl and make the creamiest, freshest, frothiest Syllabub in the world.'

· ROSEHIP SYLLABUB ·

Pare the rind off the lemon very thinly. Squeeze about 4 tablespoons of juice from the lemon and add this together with the rind to the wine. Leave the wine overnight. Remove the rind. Add the sugar and stir until dissolved. Whip the cream until it stands in peaks. Fold into the wine and lemon mixture. Spoon it into wine glasses, piling it high over the rim. Chill before serving. Decorate with very thin slices of lemon, quartered. *Serves 3–4.*

Marshmallows

275 g (10 oz) sugar
150 ml ($\frac{1}{4}$ pint) water
$\frac{1}{4}$ teaspoon cream of tartar
20 g ($\frac{3}{4}$ oz) gelatine
2 egg whites, stiffly beaten
vanilla essence
cornflour
icing sugar

Dissolve the sugar in some of the water and stir in the cream of tartar. Bring to the boil. Boil until a temperature of 260°F or 128°C is reached.

Meanwhile, dissolve the gelatine in the rest of the water. Pour the syrup on to the gelatine mixture and then fold in gradually the stiffly beaten egg whites. Add the vanilla essence and continue beating until thick. Lightly oil a tin. Dust with icing sugar. Pour in the mixture. Leave to set. When firm, loosen along the edges and turn out on to lots of icing sugar.

Cut into squares with scissors. Toss in a mixture of cornflour and icing sugar.

Coffee Carrageen Mould

600 ml (1 pint) milk
25 g (1 oz) carrageen moss
3 teaspoons instant coffee
sugar to taste – approximately 12 g
($\frac{1}{2}$ oz)

Carrageen abounds all along the Atlantic coasts of Ireland. It is high in iodine and potassium and its health-giving properties have for long made it a choice food. Also known as Pig's Wrack, it is used commercially in the production of icecream, fruit juices, etc. It is also used in a medicinal preparation for the treatment of stomach ulcers.

Wash the moss thoroughly and soak for an hour or so in cold water before using. Drain, put to boil with milk and let it barely simmer until the milk begins to thicken and coats the back of a spoon. This should take about 20 minutes. Add the coffee and sugar to taste. Stir well until dissolved. Pour into a wetted mould and allow to set. Turn out when set and serve with whipped cream. *Serves 4–6.*

Butterscotch

450 g (1 lb) sugar
150 ml ($\frac{1}{4}$ pint) water
$\frac{1}{4}$ teaspoon cream of tartar
75 g (3 oz) butter
$\frac{1}{2}$ teaspoon vanilla essence

Dissolve the sugar in the water in a heavy-bottomed saucepan over a very low heat. Stir in the cream of tartar; boil briskly until the jam-making thermometer reads 240°F, or 115°C. Slice the butter thinly and add to the mixture with the vanilla essence. Continue boiling until a temperature of 280°F or 138°C is reached. Wait a minute or so until the bubbles subside. Pour into a greased tin, making a 0.6 cm ($\frac{1}{4}$ inch) thick layer. Score deeply into squares before it cools and store in an airtight jar.

95

Irish Cranachan

100 g (4 oz) toasted oatmeal
300 ml (½ pint) whipped cream
1 tablespoon Irish Mist liqueur
100 g (4 oz) soft fruit (*fraughans* or
    bilberries, strawberries or
    raspberries)

Toast the oatmeal gently in a pan or under the grill until a nice golden brown. Fold the toasted oatmeal and the Irish Mist into the whipped cream. Pile into tall glasses, with the fruit alternating with the whipped cream and oatmeal mixture. *Serves 3–4.*

Iced Irish Mist

75 g (3 oz) well-flavoured honey
juice of ½ lemon
3 tablespoons Irish Mist
300 ml (½ pint) whipped cream

Warm the honey in a bowl over a pan of hot water until runny, then add the lemon juice and Irish Mist and fold in the whipped cream. Pour into an ice cream machine or ice trays and freeze until set. If using ice trays, turn the ice cream sides to middle when it begins to harden, to break up the ice crystals. *Serves 4.*

Blackberry Sorbet

450 g (1lb) ripe blackberries
100 g (4 oz) sugar
150 ml (¼ pint) water
dessertspoon lemon juice
few dessertspoons kirsch (optional)
2 egg whites

Sieve the blackberries. Boil the sugar and water together for 5 minutes to make a syrup. When it is cool add the blackberry purée and flavour with the lemon juice and the kirsch if wished.

    Beat the egg whites stiffly, fold them into the sorbet, and freeze as for the Iced Irish Mist above. *Serves 4.*

To make an Ice Bowl

Take two bowls, one about double the capacity of the other. Half fill the big bowl with cold water. Float the second bowl inside the first so that its rim is ½ inch above the rim of the big bowl. Place a square of fabric over the top and tie it on with string under the rim of the lower bowl. Adjust the small bowl to a central position. Put the bowls in a deep freeze. After 24 hours turn out as follows. Remove the cloth. Twist and shake the small bowl free of the ice bowl. Dip the big bowl for a second or two in warm water. Twist and shake the ice bowl free, and turn it out carefully.

· IRISH CRANACHAN ·

Gooseberry Cream

450 g (1 lb) gooseberries
175 g (6 oz) caster sugar
4 egg yolks, beaten

Gooseberry bushes seem to have been indigenous to Ireland and northern Europe. The berry was traditionally served with goose, hence its name.

Wash, top and tail the gooseberries. Put them in a saucepan with a little cold water and simmer gently until soft. Rub through a fine sieve. Stir in the caster sugar and beaten egg yolks. Cook in a double saucepan (or in a saucepan in a pan of water on the fire) stirring all the time, for a few minutes until the egg yolks are cooked. Great care must be taken that it doesn't boil or the eggs will curdle. Serve cold with whipped cream. *Serves 4–6.*

Pears in Red Wine

150 ml ($\frac{1}{4}$ pint) red wine
100 g (4 oz) caster sugar
1 clove
4 pears, not too ripe
1 heaped teaspoon arrowroot
25 g (1 oz) flaked almonds

Pour the wine and 150 ml ($\frac{1}{4}$ pint) of cold water into a saucepan. Add the sugar and clove. Heat gently to dissolve the sugar, then bring to the boil. Boil for 10–15 minutes until syrupy. Peel the pears. Using the coffee spoon or a sharp knife, remove the cores from the base, keeping the pears intact. Place the pears in the syrup, and spoon it over them. Cover the pan and simmer gently until tender, basting with the syrup from time to time. Blend the arrowroot with a little water. Remove the pears from the syrup and stand upright in a serving dish. Pour the hot syrup on the arrowroot. Stir well and return to the pan. Bring to the boil, stirring well all the time. Boil for three minutes and pour over the pears. May be served either hot or cold. *Serves 4.*

Custard Sauce

600 ml (1 pint) milk
2 egg yolks
12 g ($\frac{1}{2}$ oz) sugar
a few drops of almond, cinnamon or vanilla flavouring

Remember the old saying that 'a custard boiled is a custard spoiled'.

Boil the milk. Beat the eggs well with the sugar and the almond or other flavouring, and stir in the milk. Pour the custard into a double saucepan or a jug standing in a pan of boiling water, and stir over a moderate heat until the mixture thickens. Only allow to heat enough to thicken the eggs. (Curdling temperature is just below boiling-point, hence it is important that the mixture is never allowed to boil.)

Raspberry Delight

450 g (1 lb) raspberries
900 ml (1½ pints) water
275 g (10 oz) sugar
25 g (1 oz) cornflour

Raspberries were one of the delights enjoyed by the Fianna!

Remove stalks from the fruit, then wash and rub through a sieve. Put the water and sugar into a saucepan and boil until syrupy. Cool a little of the syrup slightly and blend with the cornflour. Stir into the rest of the syrup and bring to the boil again. Cook for a few minutes until the cornflour is cooked and the syrup has a nice clear raspberry colour. Add the fruit purée, pour into a serving dish and serve cold. *Serves 3–4.*

Irish Whiskey Trifle

225 g (8 oz) sponge cake
4 – 6 tablespoons raspberry or
  strawberry jam
100 g (4 oz) fresh or tinned fruit
  salad
1 glass Irish whiskey
300 ml (½ pint) custard

Split the sponge cake in two. Spread the slices with jam, sandwich them together again, then cut into pieces and place in a glass bowl. Sprinkle the fruit salad over the sponge. Pour the Irish whiskey over all. Coat the lot with good custard and allow to cool. *Serves 4–6.*

If liked, decorate with angelica and blobs of whipped cream for an Irish green, white and gold finish!

Honeyed Cinnamon Pears

25–50 g (1–2 oz) sugar
300 ml (½ pint) water
a little lemon juice
4 pears
225 g (8 oz) Irish honey
1½ teaspoons cinnamon

Dissolve the sugar in the water and bring to the boil. Boil for a minute or two. Add a squeeze of lemon juice. Either tinned or fresh pears may be used for this dessert. Peel and halve fresh pears and poach in sugary syrup until tender. Remove and drain. Place in the refrigerator for several hours before using. When ready to serve, heat the honey with the cinnamon. When almost boiling, pour over the cold pears and serve immediately. *Serves 4.*

Wicklow Heather Honey and Nut Pancake

100 g (4 oz) flour
½ teaspoon salt
3 eggs

Sift the flour and salt together. Add the eggs and beat flour, salt and eggs well together. Gradually add the milk, melted butter and the grating of

450 ml (¾ pint) milk
a grating of lemon rind
25 g (1 oz) butter, melted

For the filling
25 g (1 oz) walnuts
50 g (2 oz) hazelnuts
25 g (1 oz) almonds
225 g (8 oz) honey
juice of ½ lemon
a little butter

lemon rind. Allow the batter to stand for at least 1 hour before using. Prepare the filling by shelling and finely chopping the nuts. Mix them well with the honey and the lemon juice.

Heat a little butter in a pan. Ladle out just enough of the pancake mixture to barely cover the bottom of the pan. When the underside is cooked, toss. When both sides are nicely browned, put a generous spoonful of the honey mixture on the pancake. Fold in three, dust with caster sugar and serve immediately. *Serves 6.*

Cottage Cheese Cream

450 g (1 lb) cottage cheese
75 g (3 oz) butter
150 g (5 oz) sugar
a few drops of vanilla essence
300 ml (½ pint) whipped cream
45 ml (3 tablespoons) rum
3 eggs, separated
225 g (8 oz) fruit

Use redcurrants, bilberries (or *fraughans* as they are called in Ireland), strawberries, raspberries or any fruit, tinned or fresh, to make this dessert.

Sieve the cottage cheese and blend in the butter, sugar, a few drops of vanilla essence, 3 tablespoons of the whipped cream and the rum, and whisk well together. Then add the egg yolks and the stiffly beaten whites. Pile the cream and the fruit into a serving bowl and decorate with the rest of the whipped cream. *Serves 4.*

Cottage Cheese Pie

450 g (1 lb) cottage cheese
50 g (2 oz) sugar
225 g (8 oz) honey
4 eggs
175 g (6 oz) shortcrust pastry
cinnamon

Mix the cheese, sugar and honey well together in a bowl. Whisk the eggs and beat into the cheese mixture. Line a greased baking tin with the pastry and spoon in the filling. Bake in a moderate oven (350°F, Gas 4, 180°C) for 30 minutes or until golden brown. Dust the top well with cinnamon. Cool and cut into squares for serving. *Serves 6.*

Yellowman (traditional)

Cinnamon buttons and yellowman
And brandy balls in a bright tin can.

25 g (1 oz) butter
450 g (1 lb) golden syrup
2 tablespoons water
1 teaspoon baking soda
225 g (½ lb) brown sugar

Aunt Jane's cupboards were always well stocked with the coveted delights. At the Lammas Fair on the first of August in Ballycastle, Co. Antrim, a character called Dick Murray earned immortality and renown because every Fair day he made and sold a variety of yellowman guaranteed to cure all diseases. I'm not sure if this is his recipe or not!

Grease a large dish with the butter. Dissolve the sugar with the syrup and water in a large saucepan over a gentle heat. Boil without stirring until a drop becomes crisp when dropped in cold water. Then you are ready to move on to the next stage. (If you have a sugar thermometer for jam-making, the mixture should be crisp at about 290°F (or 140°C). Next, stir in the baking soda and pour into the large greased dish. Fold in the edges to the centre and as soon as it is cool enough to handle, pull the mixture, stretching it as much as you can. Fold in the edges to the centre again and pull. Continue folding and pulling until the sheet of toffee is a light yellowish colour. Break up into bite-sized chunks and store in an airtight jar or leave in long twists

Dublin Rock

This is a rich decorative pudding fashionable in the 1880s and 1890s, and comes courtesy of Theodora Fitzgibbon and her charming book *A Taste of Ireland* (J.M. Dent and Pan Books). As she remarks, it must indeed have looked very ornate on the long dining tables of the period.

Make an earthenware mixing bowl very hot, and put into it the butter or cream. Beat into this the almonds and sugar, and when well mixed add the brandy and a few drops of orange flower water (this can usually be bought at a chemist). Continue the beating until the bowl is quite cold, then add the stiffly beaten egg whites and amalgamate well (nowadays this could all be done in an electric blender). Leave the mixture overnight in a cold place until it is quite stiff. Break into rough pieces (it will be soft but firm) and pile onto a glass dish in the shape of a pyramid.

Decorate with strips of green angelica, shredded blanched almonds and, as in the old days, little fronds of maidenhair fern to resemble plants, such as shamrock, growing out of a rock.

. C I N N A M O N   B U T T O N S .

4 oz butter or 1 cup very thick
   cream
2 stiffly beaten egg whites
a few drops of orange flower water
½ lb ground almonds
2 oz caster sugar
1 tablespoon brandy
angelica, blanched split almonds
   and maidenhair fern for
   decoration

Cinnamon Buttons

25 g (1 oz) cinnamon

Mix the cinnamon and sugar thoroughly together.

450 g (1 lb) sugar
2 egg whites, stiffly beaten
300 ml (½ pint) water

Add the stiffly beaten egg whites and the water, mixing all together. Drop the mixture from a spoon on to aluminium foil or on to a lightly greased tin. Dry in a very cool oven, 250°F, Gas ½, 130°C.

Rhubarb and Apple Crunch

225 g (8 oz) cooking apples, peeled
  and chopped
450 g (1 lb) rhubarb
juice and grated rind of 1 lemon
2 tablespoons cornflour
450 ml (¾ pint) milk
2 eggs
¼ teaspoon vanilla essence
2 tablespoons honey
100 g (4 oz) butter
100 g (4 oz) oatmeal
1 teaspoon mixed spice
75 g (3 oz) brown sugar

Stew the apple, rhubarb, lemon juice and teaspoon of rind until soft. Arrange in a shallow, greased, ovenproof dish. Blend the cornflour in a little milk. Add to the remainder of the milk and bring to the boil. Cook gently for about 10 minutes. Take the sauce off the heat, whisk the eggs and add them to it. Stir in the honey and the vanilla essence. Pour the sauce over the apple and the rhubarb. Melt the butter in a pan, add the oatmeal, mixed spice and sugar. Stir over a low heat for a few minutes to dissolve the sugar and partly cook the oatmeal. Spoon over the sauce and bake in a moderately hot oven (400°F, Gas 6, 200°C) for 20 minutes. *Serves 6.*

Junket

A traveller in Limerick in 1690 tells us 'These people are the greatest lovers of milk I ever saw. They eat and drink about twenty different milk dishes and strangest of all, they love it best when it is sourest.' Buttermilk, known as *bainne clabair* and referred to by writers in English as 'bonnyclabber' was popular: according to some, 'the bravest, freshest drink you ever tasted'. Junket was probably also appreciated, since rennet was much used from ancient times.

600 ml (1 pint) milk
25 g (1 oz) sugar
1 dessertspoon liquid rennet
a few drops of vanilla essence
a grating of cinnamon or nutmeg

Put the milk in a pan and warm to blood heat. Add the sugar, rennet and vanilla essence and stir well. Pour into the individual dessert dishes in which it is to be brought to table – it tends to turn to whey once it is cut – and grate a little cinnamon or nutmeg over each. Serve with fruit. *Serves 4–6.*
  Junket may be varied by mixing a little coffee essence with a small amount of the milk and then adding to the rest. A spoonful of cocoa makes a pleasant flavouring also.

· JUNKET ·

DRINKS AND COCKTAILS

It is a little known fact, but none the less true, that Ireland can proudly claim the 'cocktail', that status symbol of the Scott Fitzgerald era, as her invention. Betsy Flanagan took the dreaded emigrant boat for America when the Famine in Ireland was at its very worst. She followed her ten brothers, leaving a heart-broken mother in the West of Ireland. She was an out-going, big-hearted lass who very quickly put the past behind her and settled into life in New England. She got a job in a tavern. In 1779, war was raging in America, and Betsy's tavern became the meeting place for the French and American officers of George Washington's army. Despite the strains of camp life and war, the merriment at Betsy's tavern knew no bounds. One day, as an added diversion for her boys, Betsy served up one of her Tory farmer neighbour's prized cockerels for dinner. When the soldiers adjourned to the bar to continue the festivities, they found that Betsy had decorated the bottles with feathers from the Tory farmer's roosters. A delighted French soldier proposed the toast 'Vive le cocktail!' (His knowledge of English grammar was weak!) The cocktail was born. From then on, concoctions made from different drinks have been known as cocktails – and all thanks to an Irish lass!

The Irish have always taken their drinking seriously and appreciated a well-aged, mellow beverage. From earliest times, mead and beer seem to have been appreciated. An ancient chieftain, welcoming Fionn Mac Cumhaill, assured him 'I shall give you what is oldest in every drink and newest in every food.' Fionn himself entertained with a hundred measures of 'coal-black drink'. Is this where Guinness, founder of Ireland's – indeed, of Europe's – largest brewery, got his inspiration?

Very early on, clarets and Spanish wines were imported for special occasions. Dean Swift preferred Bishop, a hot, spicy punch. Later, we hear that 'Spanish wine shall give you hope, my dark Rosaleen'. The humble sloe was also much prized. We know that the monks in Holy Cross Abbey in Co. Tipperary produced a kind of gin. Gin of sorts seems to have been common enough, so not surprisingly we find in the south of Ireland a Church of the Sloes (Killarney – *Cill Airne*). However, French wines were undoubtedly the most prized drink, and from earliest times, vast quantities of claret and of other wines were imported directly from Bordeaux and Tours. By the eighteenth century, very close links existed between Bordeaux and Ireland so that we find Swift writing with amazement to his girl-friend Stella, that while claret in Dublin was only 2/6d (12½p) a bottle, the 'basest wine in London' cost 6/- (30p) a bottle. Swift was probably expressing the feeling of his contemporaries when he wrote 'Wine is the liquor of the gods; ale of the Goths.'

Whiskey was a comparative late-comer on the scene. Somewhere around 1405 we come across the story of a man who paradoxically killed himself with over-consumption of whiskey, *uisce-beatha*, the water of life. The ancient Bard is mightily puzzled by this strange state of affairs. By the time of the reign of Queen Elizabeth I, Irish whiskey was already famous and a traveller of the times notes that it is certainly the best whiskey in the world. Peter the Great of Russia leaves it on record that of all the beverages in the world, Irish Usquebaugh is the best. In 1728, Swift writes to enquire whether Lady Bolingbroke would prefer green or yellow whiskey for, he assures her, 'there is no such thing as white'. Seemingly in those days whiskey was a pure alcohol mixed with flavourings like saffron, nutmeg and sugar. Green whiskey was never dependable: aged, it tended to lose its colour, while when it was young, it was very fiery and hot.

The emigrant Irish took with them their happy skill in this area. Bourbon whisky was first made in America by despairing Irish emigrants trying to capture the taste of the drink so dear to them in their native land! The Comte de Hennessy's ancestors adapted their talents in the south-west of France and the result is one of the world's finest cognacs. One doesn't have to search too far to guess the origins of Château Kirwan, or of Château Lynch-Bages in the Gironde, but what about Château Haut-Brion? Many people believe that it is a gallicisation of a good Irish name, O'Brien.

Lord Dunsany notices another aspect of Irish drinking habits: 'They appreciate occasional stimulants of whiskey, sport and politics. For choice, Irishmen prefer all three refined and purified from any alloy of the law, as for instance when the whiskey is poteen, brewed in a bog out of sight of the Law's representatives and paying no duty to them.' Or in the words of an old song:

What more diversion can a man desire
Than to seat him down by an ale-house fire
Upon his knee a pretty wench
And on the table a jug of punch?

Another darker side emerges however, from another popular song

Whiskey, you're the devel
You're driving me insane. . . .

Carrageen Drink

25 g (1 oz) carrageen
1.8 litres (3 pints) milk
a pinch of salt
fresh lemon rind or other desired
    flavouring
sugar to taste

For bronchitis, ulcers, 'flu or just plain exhaustion, this iodine and sulphur rich drink is irreplaceable. Even the weakest stomachs can tolerate it and it's a pleasant drink into the bargain!

Wash and trim the carrageen and steep for at least an hour. Stain it and put it into a saucepan with the milk and salt. Bring to the boil and simmer for about 4 or 5 hours. 20 minutes or so before the end of cooking, add a few chips of lemon rind and sugar to taste. Strain and serve piping hot.

Lemon and Orange Whey

600 ml (1 pint) milk
juice of 1 orange or 2 tablespoons
    lemon juice

In 1691 a visitor called Petty notes that 'the diet of these people is milk, sweet and sour, thick and thin, which also is their drink in Summertime'.

Add the orange or lemon juice to the milk. Stand at room temperature for an hour or so. Then chill thoroughly. Drink both curds and whey. If you like yogurt, you will find this a most refreshing and health-giving drink.

Sloe Gin

225 g (8 oz) sloes
225 g (8 oz) sugar
Gin

Wash the sloes and prick all over with a pin to release juices. Mix with sugar. Half-fill a bottle with this mixture and top up with gin. Cork tightly and leave for at least three months before drinking.

Metheglin or Mead

25 g (1 oz) yeast
1 tablet of yeast nutrient (optional)
2.7 kg (6 lb) honey
9.6 litres (2 gallons) water

From earliest times, mead was probably the commonest drink in Ireland.

Mead is a variation on a simple country wine, so if you have made any wine, you should have no difficulty at all. Put the yeast and starter in a bottle with a little lukewarm water. Cork the bottle with a cotton wool plug and leave in a warm place until the yeast starts to bubble and foam vigorously. Meanwhile, add the honey to the water and bring to

·MEAD·

the boil. Skim off, and allow to cool until lukewarm. Stir in the yeast mixture and pour the lot into a fermentation jar. Do not fill to the brim, to allow room for the mixture to froth. Fit a cotton wool plug for a day or two until the initial fermentation subsides. Then fit a cork with an airlock, as for wine-making. Keep in a warm place (65°F–75°F, 18°C–24°C) until the fermentation stops. Syphon into storage jars and store in a cool place for about a year, if possible, before bottling and using.

Sloe Gin Rickey

1 cube of ice
juice of ½ lime
50 ml (2 fl.oz) sloe gin

Put all the ingredients into a 225 ml (8 fl.oz) highball glass. Top up with soda water and stir.

Irish Widow's Dream Cocktail

30 ml (2 tablespoons) Irish Mist liqueur
1 whole egg
1 teaspoon cream

Shake the Irish Mist and egg well with cracked ice and strain into a 100 ml (4 fl.oz) cocktail glass. Float the cream on top and serve immediately.

Scailtin

150 ml (¼ pint) hot milk
12 g (½ oz) butter
12 g (½ oz) sugar
small piece of cinnamon or a few cloves
50 ml (2 fl.oz) Irish whiskey

(traditional: pronounced *Skol-teen*)

Heat cinnamon or cloves in milk until about to boil. Add butter and sugar and stir well until thoroughly dissolved. Put Irish whiskey in a heated tumbler. Pour milk mixture over and serve immediately.

Black Velvet

300 ml (½ pint) Guinness
300 ml (½ pint) champagne

Black Velvet is the artist's drink! James Joyce in his *A Portrait of the Artist as A Young Man* shows a predilection for this cocktail. His interest in Guinness (as in all things of Dublin) was a lasting one and at a later stage he even entered a slogan competition run by them and was disappointed not to win with this apostrophe, as heady in its way as the pint of Guinness he addresses 'That's my old Dublin *lindubh*, the free, the fro the frothy freshener!' *Lindubh*, typically,

105

is a Joycean pun on the Irish words which mean 'black pool' – as well as a reversal of the syllables in Dublin. Time for a Black Velvet after all that!

Pour chilled Guinness and iced champagne simultaneously into a large tumbler and serve immediately.

Irish Rickey

1 cube of ice
juice of ½ lemon
30 ml (2 tablespoons) Irish
    whiskey

Put all the ingredients together into a 225 ml (8 fl.oz) highball glass. Top up with soda water and stir.

Everybody's Irish Cocktail

5 ml (1 teaspoon) Crème de
    Menthe
5 ml (1 teaspoon) Green
    Chartreuse
50 ml (2 fl.oz) Irish Whiskey

Stir the ingredients well together with cracked ice. Strain into a cocktail glass.

Oisin's Delight

15 ml (1 tablespoon) vermouth
30 ml (2 tablespoons) Irish
    whiskey
1 teaspoon Irish Mist
a twist of lemon

Stir the ingredients well with cracked ice and strain into a cocktail glass. Decorate with a twist of lemon.

Lemonade

3 lemons
75 g (3 oz) sugar
900 ml (1½ pints) cold water

Peel the lemons very thinly, taking care not to include any of the white pith. A potato peeler is handy for this. Put the lemon rind in a large earthenware jug with the sugar. Allow to stand for about 1 hour – by then, the sugar should have drawn the oils from the rind. Stir the sugar into the cold water. Squeeze the juice from the lemons and strain. Add the cold water and stir well with a wooden spoon. Leave in the refrigerator or in a cool place for about 24 hours. Strain, discarding the lemon rind, and serve chilled.

Paddy Mint Julep

1 teaspoon sugar
sprig of fresh mint
crushed ice
1 measure Paddy Irish whiskey

Dissolve the sugar in a little water in a 350 ml (12 fl.oz) glass. Crush a leaf of mint in the sugary water and leave it there. Pack the glass with crushed ice. Add Paddy whiskey. Stir well. Decorate with a few pieces of mint leaf.

Bushmills Whiskey Sour

20 ml ($\frac{1}{2}$ jigger) lemon and lime juice
40 ml (1 jigger) Bushmills whiskey
1 teaspoon caster sugar
cracked ice
cherry and slice of orange for decoration

Put cracked ice in the bottom of a glass. Add lemon and lime juice, Bushmills whiskey and caster sugar. Stir well and serve decorated with a cherry and a slice of orange.

Irish Coffee

A double measure of Irish whiskey
5 ml (1 teaspoon) brown sugar
70 ml (4 tablespoons) lightly whipped cream
$\frac{3}{4}$ glass hot, black, strong coffee

Put the sugar into a warmed, stemmed glass. Fill the glass three-quarters full of coffee. Add plenty of Irish whiskey. Top off with cream. Float it on to the surface over the back of a spoon and do not stir. Drink the hot strong coffee through the cool cream.
Slainte!

Bishop

1 orange, quartered
1 blade mace
8 cloves
1 stick of cinnamon
$\frac{1}{4}$ teaspoon allspice
2 bottles Port wine

This was a favourite drink of Dean Swift.

Put all the spices in 300 ml ($\frac{1}{2}$ pint) of water and simmer gently until the liquid is reduced by half. Strain. Put the strained liquid in a larger saucepan with the orange. Add the port wine and heat thoroughly but on no account let it boil.

If desired, add about a cocktail-glassful of brandy just before serving.

Strain into warmed punch glasses to serve.

Wild-eyed Rose Highball

juice of $\frac{1}{2}$ lime
50 ml (2 fl.oz) Irish whiskey
1 cube of ice
soda water

Mix all the ingredients in a 225 ml (8 fl.oz) highball glass. Top up with soda water and stir gently.

Mulled Red Wine

9 bottles elderberry or sloe wine
2 lemons, very thinly sliced
1 cup sugar
600 ml (1 pint) water
4 sticks cinnamon
4 cloves
1 to 2 glasses of poteen, if available

My thanks go to Desmond Egan for this recipe.

Boil the water, sugar, cinnamon and cloves together for 5 minutes. Then add the very thinly sliced lemons. Cover and let stand for about 10 minutes to bring out and blend the different flavours.
  Add the wine and poteen and heat gradually. Take care the mixture doesn't boil once the wine has been added.
  Serve very hot. *Serves 6.*

Grog

1 measure of Jamaican rum
1 teaspoon sugar
2 cloves
juice of half a lemon
piece of cinnamon stick

Heat a tumbler well. Put all the ingredients in together and top up with boiling water.

Jameson's Toddy

1 measure Jameson's whiskey
1 teaspoon sugar
2 cloves
1 slice of lemon
1 small stick of cinnamon

Heat glass well. Put in all the ingredients and fill up with boiling water.

Irish Shillelagh

juice of ½ lemon
1 teaspoon caster sugar
40 ml (jigger) Irish whiskey
15 ml (1 tablespoon) sloe gin
15 ml (1 tablespoon) rum
1 strawberry, 1 raspberry, 1 cherry

Shake well with cracked ice and strain into a 150 ml (5 fl.oz) punch glass. Decorate with a fresh raspberry, strawberry and a cherry.

St Patrick's Day Cocktail

15 ml (1 tablespoon) Crème de Menthe
15 ml (1 tablespoon) Green Chartreuse
15 ml (1 tablespoon) Irish whiskey
1 dash bitters

Stir well with cracked ice and strain into a 75 ml (3 fl.oz) cocktail glass.

15 ml (1 tablespoon) vermouth
30 ml (2 tablespoons) Irish
   whiskey
1 dash orange bitters

Rory O'Moore

Stir well with cracked ice and strain into a 75 ml (3 fl.oz) cocktail glass.

2 parts sloe gin
1 part vermouth
1 dash orange bitters
lemon peel

Blackthorn Special

Put all the ingredients into a glass with crushed ice. Stir until really cold and strain into a cocktail glass.

40 ml (1 jigger) of Irish whiskey
15 ml (1 tablespoon) French
   vermouth
1 teaspoon Crème de Menthe

Shamrock Cocktail

Stir the ingredients together with cracked ice and strain into a 75 ml (3 fl.oz) cocktail glass. Serve with green olives.

70 ml (4 tablespoons) Sherry
dash of bitters
orange peel

Sherry Cocktail

Stir well with cracked ice and strain into 350 ml (12 fl.oz) Tom Collins glass. Twist a small piece of orange peel to release the rich oils in rind and drop into the glass.

SHERRY COCKTAIL

CHOICE
OLD
FULL PALE
SHERRY

Index